Complete Guide to Group Discussion

COMPLETE GUIDE TO GROUP DISCUSSION

Krishan Kumar

The Readers Paradise
New Delhi - 110002

Complete Guide to Group Discussion
Krishan Kumar

First Edition

ISBN - 978-81-938231-1-8

Published by
The Readers Paradise
103, 4787/23, Ansari Road,
Darya Ganj, New Delhi - 110002
09654444181
thereadersparadisesales@gmail.com
www.thereadersparadise.com

Price Rs. 995.00

Page No. - 202 | Paper - 80gsm
Size - 5.5x8.5

Typesetting & Cover Design by
Sanya Computers

Printed at Apac Business Solution Pvt. Ltd.
Darya Ganj, New Delhi - 110002

Preface

Why do so many world-changing insights come from people with little or no related experience? Charles Darwin was a geologist when he proposed the theory of evolution. And it was an astronomer who finally explained what happened to the dinosaurs. Frans Johansson's The Medici Effect shows how breakthrough ideas most often occur when we bring concepts from one field into a new, unfamiliar territory and offers examples of how we can turn the ideas we discover into path-breaking innovations. Clayton M. Christensen, bestselling author of The Innovator's Dilemma, has described The Medici Effect as "one of the most insightful books about managing innovation I have ever read. Its assertion that breakthrough principles of creativity occur at novel intersections is an enduring principle of creativity that should guide innovators in every field."

Every year, after successfully crossing the first hurdle (the MBA entrance exams), MBA aspirants immediately face the next hurdle in the path to their dream B-schools – the Group Discussions (GD) & Personal Interviews (PI).

These stages of the selection process give the selection committee of the B-schools a deeper insight into a candidate's personality.

During a GD a candidate's understanding of the topic, attitude, self-confidence, presence of mind and leadership skills are put to the test. Inadequate preparation can often sabotage a GD.

In a PI time is of the essence. Creating an impact within the limited time frame under pressure plays an important role here. Every candidate needs to be well prepared before facing the panellists.

To help our students through this daunting task, here is a book that explains exactly what to expect in a GD/PI. The material in this book outlines each step of the selection process and throws light on what is expected of a student at a GD/PI.

The compilation of theory lessons, articles by CAT 100 percentiles, user experiences and GD capsules in this book will boost a candidate's GD/PI preparation. This book aims at providing students with the extra edge and confidence needed to crack the GD/PI session and secure a seat in a coveted B-school.

Foreword

English has become a global language. In the minds of many worldwide, it guarantees a better life through enhanced social and economic opportunities. As a result, English teachers are in high demand. Some claim that English is attractive because as it has spread throughout the world, it has severed its ties from any specific culture, making it easily malleable to fit the needs of those who adopt it. Grammar rules and vocabulary can simply be taught to eager learners so they can use English for social and economic advancement.

However, learning English is more than mastering a certain number of words and memorizing a set of grammar rules. Although plugging words into scientific formulas might be the key to success in chemistry or physics, it is less effective for language learners. Language acquisition studies have discovered that both native and non native speakers learn English best not by being taught rules but by interacting with other users of the language, either orally or through print. This interaction introduces a social element to grammar that brings with it hidden social messages.

The systematic ways in which the meaning expressed by group discussion rules is changes according to social settings is called pragmatics. The rules governing the expected sequence of sentences in a conversation or a composition according to pragmatic conditions fall under the rubric of discourse. In other words, if English language learners want to use English to better themselves, they need to know more than grammar. They need to know how pragmatics and discourse affect their choice of grammar rules as they interact with other English speakers if they want to avoid misunderstandings. Teachers who are preparing their students to interact with other users of English by combining grammar with pragmatics and discourse are teaching them communicative competence. The lessons in this book reflect the many teacher training workshops and grammar classes that I have taught in Mexico, Hungary, and the Philippines as well as in Florida, Texas, and other parts of the United States over the last thirty years. They shed new light on English grammar by including the results from research in second language acquisition, sociolinguistics, pragmatics, and discourse analysis in ways that are accessible to those who have a limited background in linguistics.

Contents

1

Introduction

Real time demonstration of behavioural skills is the basic rationale behind the inclusion of group discussion as one of the selection techniques. None of the other techniques test the candidate's managerial skills like communication skills, knowledge and ideas regarding a given subject, capability to co-ordinate and lead, etc. as well as a group discussion. Involvement of strangers in the discussion, lower familiarity with the GD topic and limited preparation time makes the job easier for the selection panel while making things difficult for the candidates.

A group discussion, involves speaking before a group of people. This puts in some aspects of public speaking i.e. speaking and content. However, due to its interactive nature, a group discussion also involves listening to other people's ideas. A typical group discussion has 8-12 participants and lasts for 15 to 20 minutes. It means each participant gets an average of around 2 minutes to talk; the rest of the time is spent listening.

Consequently, group discussion preparation revolves around these three basic aspects.

GROUP SPEAKING PREPARATION

In a group discussion, a candidate should be able to convey his/her thoughts satisfactorily and convincingly before a group of people. Knowledge on a given subject, precision and clarity of thought are the things that are evaluated. One should speak only as much as necessary and try to avoid irrelevant talks and being verbose.

1. To enhance fluency, tone of voice and articulation, start by reading aloud from a book or an editorial for around 15 minutes daily. Once a week, try speaking in front of a mirroron some topic. This would also help in collecting your thoughts in an organized manner.
2. Most of us may be very vocal in a one – to – one conversation but are less so when interact with a group; especially if it is a group of strangers. So, start having some discussions with a group made from your friends. Such discussions are a good way to begin as they allow students to focus on speaking without being distracted by the extremely competitive environment of a formal group discussion.
3. After content preparation for one or two weeks, start attending competitive group discussions with likeminded groups.

GROUP CONTENT PREPARATION

Presence of content will be a primary determinant of how you perform in any group discussion. If you are making a content heavy point, especially with some facts and numbers, then everybody else will listen to what you have to say. This generally helps in making subsequent entries in the discussion. For someone who keeps himself updated with current affairs, content preparation may not be an issue.

For others, I advise the following:

1. Pick around 6 – 7 current affair topics, (events that took place in the past year) and start researching on these. Understand the event from different perspectives like personal,social, political, cultural, academic etc.
2. While reading magazines or newspapers, focus should primarily be on well covered articles or stories. Reading articles from the Sunday Express, the Mint, Business Standard and the Economist is a good preparation for group discussions. One may also look at some blogs that contain a few well researched articles.
3. While researching on topics, try to remember important facts and figures and form some opinions with justification.
4. In many discussions ranging from the recession to China as a threat to India foroutsourcing; comparison between India and

China or US is inevitable. So, it is advisableto know a lot of economic and demographic details of these countries like GDP, population, social structure, major industries etc.

GROUP LISTENING PREPARATION

A crucial but ignored part of group discussion preparation is listening. Often, we undermine benefits of listening. A good listener would summarize discussions well; he/she may score by presenting a good case over an idea originated by another participant but lost in high decibel noise. Listening seems very easy; but what takes some preparation is to be able to listen and at the same time, structure your own thoughts.

1. Participate in some discussions as an observer. Listening exercise during such practice discussions would help you understand the dynamics of a typical GD that involves high-low noise levels. Such an exercise would provide you with some hints as to optimum moments for entering discussions.
2. Listening to other people's ideas may help to evolve one's thought processes by adding different perspectives.

GROUP DISCUSSION TIPS

1. In a discussion, if you talk in a long-winded way, then the other participants will not becourteous and wait for you to come to the point. Hence, speaking in a concise manner isvery important
2. Address everyone in the group so while you are making your point you are not talking to one person only but the whole group. At the same time, do not look at the moderators asthey are not a part of the group.
3. Dress formally and use formal language.
4. Address other participants with respect. Do not gesticulate a lot; if you are accustomedto using your hands while making a point ensure that you do not encroach into the spacein front of other participants.
5. Do not point to a specific participant while talking. Do not get personal; try to beobjective in your arguments.
6. Avoid using extreme words and extreme statements.
7. If you are disagreeing with someone else do it civilly. Disagree with the point and not with the person.

1. Personal Preparation

Knowing yourself is the most important part of your interview preparation. It is not acceptable if a candidate cannot answer questions based on his/her own personality. It would give an impression of an immature or "self – unaware" person. A candidate hence needs to do a lot of soul searching on questions like: "Why MBA?", Strengths and Weaknesses, Examples of Leadership abilities, long term/ short term goals.

Projecting a consistent personality demands clarity of thoughts. So the best and easiest way to manage this is to be honest with you.

Avoid saying something like "I do not have any weakness" as it is obviously an overstatement; such an answer implies either an arrogant person or a misinformed person and the panel would not want either.

Sometimes, introspection becomes quite tricky as various qualities may coexist in bits. One should always consider the dominant quality. In such cases, feedbacks from friends and colleagues can be quite effective. Try to supplement your answers with at least two relevant examples while preparing; so that during an interview you are not unnerved if the interviewer asks you for another example. It brings additional coherency in your thoughts.

Quite a few interviews start with "Tell us something about yourself." please refrain from giving a summary of what is already written in your form / resume. Try to use this question to lead the interview into your comfort zones. For example, if you are an avid reader then you could speak about the influence of your favourite books on your character.

2. Work Experience

If you have been working for more than six months then questions on your work experience will play a role during your interview. The obvious areas of questioning are work profile, your projects, organization chart of your company and where you fit in. You should be able to give some examples of team work and leadership from your employment.

You must also focus on the macro picture of your experience in the corporate life. What it has taught you? What kind of mistakes have you made? How it has influenced to make choices in specialization for your MBA? How you have influenced the goals of your department / company? Along with this, you should also do some homework on the industry in which your company operates the history of your company, the culture of your company / industry, etc.

3. Academics

If you have been working for less than 2 years, then you are still supposed to remember some aspects of your education. Sounds scary, considering that a lot of us do not know what we are studying even when we are studying it. Do not worry; you do not need to study everything, ensure that you know the basics of all the subjects that you have studied.

A good barometer would be curriculum till higher secondary. You should also have one or two favourite subjects (If you do not have one, pick one); for these subjects you should know your curriculum and maybe a little bit more in-depth.

4. Hobbies

Ideally, hobbies should be the area of your comfort and can really make interviews quite interesting as they can clearly make a distinction between you and the rest. Most IIM graduates possess influential hobbies like reading, playing some sports, dramatics, photography, trekking etc. Watching movies and listening to music do not count as hobbies unless you can discourse on topics like directorial styles or history of various genres of music. Not having a hobby is certainly negative; but worse is getting grilled for a cited hobby when you do not have one.

5. General Knowledge / Current Affairs

General Knowledge can be a vast topic. However, this should not stop you from having opinions on current affairs. Familiarize yourself with the issue by reading magazines, blogs, and newspapers. Back your opinions with facts and justifications. Common knowledge like the capital of some countries should be known. Prepare for GK only if you have the time and have finished preparing for all the other areas.

Be systematic regarding your preparation, make a check list of what you do not know and work with it. If you are organized, you will do well in your interview. Best of Luck Commonly asked questions

I. PERSONAL

A. Background

1. Tell me about yourself.
2. What would you like me to know about you that is not on your resume?
3. What are the three most important events of your life?
4. What was an experience in your life that you would want to go back and change?

B. Self-Description

1. How would your friends describe you?
2. Give me three words to describe you.

C. Goals

1. What new goals have you established for yourself recently?
2. What are your five to ten-year career goals?
3. What are the attributes of an ideal job for you? If you could do "it" all over again, what would you do differently?

D. Values

4. What does "success" mean to you?
5. What does "failure" mean to you?
6. Which is more important to you: money or the type of job?
7. Who do you admire? Why?

II. MANAGEMENT / LEADERSHIP STYLE

1. Define leadership.
2. Tell me about a time when you successfully resolved a conflict.
3. Give me an example of a leadership role you have held when not everything went aplanned.
4. What two attributes are most important in your job?
5. How do you feel about working overtime?

Strengths / Weaknesses and Skills

1. What are your strengths/weakness?
2. Give me an example of something that you have done that shows initiative.
3. What makes you stand out among your fellow students?
4. Have you ever had any failures? What did you learn from them?

5. How do you feel about working in a structured environment?
6. In what kind of work environment do you do your best work?
7. What kinds of tasks and responsibilities motivate you the most?

Education

1. Why did you decide to get an MBA?
2. Why IIMA? (Or whichever institute you are being interviewed in.)
3. What made you decide to major in ____?
4. What electives have you taken? Which did you enjoy the most?
5. What college classes did you like the least? Why?

Extra-Curricular

1. What extra-curricular school activities are you involved in?
2. What have you learned from your activities?
3. What is your favourite book/movie/song/painting or author/actor/singer/artist?
4. Which magazines/newspapers do you read regularly? Which books have you readrecently?

Job / Company / Industry

1. What do you know about your company?
2. What do you predict is going to happen in this industry in the next 5 years?
3. Do you know who your competitors are?
4. What interests you most about this position? What parts of the job do you think youwould find the least satisfying?
5. What concerns you about your company?

The Group Discussion stage forms an integral part of the admission process to most IIMs. It tests you on several aspects. The Group Discussion is an excellent platform for you to showcase your communication skills, reasoning ability, ability to be a team player and your leadership qualities. All of these are essential to be a good manager.

The weightage that the Group Discussion carries in your final admission decision is also significant, ranging from 15-20%. More importantly, the Group Discussion is your first opportunity to make an impression on the panel that will be interviewing you later. First impressions always count, and you don't want the panel to have any negative preconceived notions about you.

The Group Discussion can follow any of several formats. Usually, the groups are of 8-11 people.

The topic is given at the start. At this point, the panel may ask you to write on the topic for 5-10 minutes and then discuss it, or to gather your thoughts for a couple of minutes and then start. In either case, there is absolutely no excuse for not carrying a pen and paper into the Group Discussion room. If you are required to start after a couple of minutes, quickly jot down some points that seem relevant to you. Concentrate on thinking of as many points as you can at this point instead of trying to frame the points in your best language. If you have more time, you can present the points in a more coherent fashion. However, remember that substance is always more important than style. This does not, of course, mean that you should write abbreviations, SMS-language, or use poor grammar, but there is no point in being unnecessarily verbose.

Group Discussion topics are of three types. The topic may be a social or political issue that the panel wants you to discuss e.g. climate change. It may also take the form of a case where you arerequired to think for a protagonist and decide on an appropriate course of action. Finally, it may be a completely abstract topic such as "Orange". A common variation in Group Discussions occurs when the panel asks you to select by consensus a topic to be discussed or asks you to choose between two topics the one you wish to discuss as a group. Remember that you are being judged even during the process of reaching a decision.

Never assume that the Group Discussion has not begun because a topic has not been selected.

Every word you speak in the Group Discussion room is on the record, as GDs are meant to simulate corporate meetings which are always painfully formal discussions in the real world.

There are some tactics that I used during my IIM GDs, which helped me a great deal. They are:

1. Pretend like its real:

In a real corporate meeting, you need to treat everyone with respect and win their respect in order to bring everyone around to your point of view. There are several things that yousimply cannot do in a real meeting that I find people do during Group Discussions, such asputting someone else down or using a casual tone of voice. Pretending like it's a real meeting will automatically make you more alert and less prone to making mistakes during the GD.

2. Treat everyone with respect:

An important attribute you will be judged on is whether you are a team player or not.

Being disdainful will therefore not help you. Be polite when dealing with opposing points of view. Try to explain with logical reasons why a person is incorrect, no matter how outrageous his line of reasoning is. Also, never ever tell someone that he is wrong.

Use softer phrases like 'That's interesting but another point of view would be...' or 'That's true in some cases but I would also like to point out that...'

3. Don't panic:

The point you were just trying to make was just stolen. The person next to you is shouting down everything you're saying. Relax. The panel judging you looks at how well you can deal with people and situations. Take a deep breath, compose yourself, think of another point and jump back into the discussion like nothing happened.

4. Forget what your GD coach taught you:

Well, not all of it, but the parts about speaking at least 6-7 times in a 15-minute GD.

Every GD is different. You can open your mouth just twice during a GD and end up looking like the best candidate in the room or make 15 points and still find yourself on the list of rejects. There are no set rules that can be framed about the number of times you should speak. Go with the flow and do what you feel comfortable doing. Quality and not quantity is what the panel is looking for. Remember though, that to get some points you need to speak at least a couple of times.

5. Get plenty of practice:

The more GDs you practice, the better you get. You can refine your style of speaking as well as your thought process with the aid of practice GDs. Practicing GDs also makes you adept athandling different types of situations and ensures that you're on top of your game when it counts. Practice both case as well as non-case GDs as you never know what the IIMs will spring on you.

6. Body Language is important, but not that important:

Most GD coaches put undue stress on your body language during a GD. While it is important to look alert during a GD, concentrating on how you look rather than on how you talk will only hamper your chances. Ensure that you do the basics of sitting up straight, looking everyone in the eye while speaking and not being too animated (e.g. waving your arms wildly about). Apart from that, make a genuine effort to listen to people. This will wipe that bored expression off your face, and stop you from twiddling your pen and staring at your shoes.

7. Don't be scared to start:

Do not hesitate to be the first one to speak, if you feel that everyone has taken sufficient time to think during the GD. The panel appreciates leadership skills. At the same time,don't just say any old thing. Be prepared with a coherent opening statement, don't ramble, and never, ever summarize the topic given to you or start off with sentences like

The LEADER in Online MBA Test Prep

"Dear Friends, we are gathered here at the GD of IIMX to discuss..." This is a formal discussion, and everybody knows why they are there.

8. Practice role-play:

For case GDs, practice writing down the names of the concerned parties and writing points from their points of view. This will help you gain a clearer understanding of the problem and help you channel your thoughts better.

9. Think before you speak:

There is no sense in shouting down someone only to blurt out half a sentence. This creates a bad impression. Mentally prepare at least a couple of sentences that you want to say. If someone cuts you off and prevent you from saying everything you wanted to, hey, at least you tried. The panel will appreciate the effort. Also, concentrate on only one point at a time. Don't try and touch on multiple points during a single foray into the GD, as chances are that not only will the second point not be heard, it will also be stolen by someone else.

10. Remember the summary:

Many IIMs require you to write a GD summary. Those don't usually ask students for an oral summary. This is a great chance to make a good impression on the panel in a safe environment away from the bustle of a GD, as the panel gives their undivided attention to one candidate at a time. Therefore, never lose track of the GD in the rush to speak andtry and always have an overall 'feel' of where the discussion is heading.

11. Read:

Finally, it helps to keep abreast of the news of the world and the country. People quoting facts and figures during a GD create a fantastic impression if the figures are accurate and relevant. Even if the figures are slightly inaccurate, as opposed to blatantly ridiculous, they ensure the speaker a chance to be heard, as people usually respect someone who they perceive to have a deeper knowledge of the topic. A person who is well-read can expect to encounter few topics which alien to him are, which is a huge advantage in a GD.

The most important things in a GD are your maturity and confidence. When you speak, take your time. Try and show restraint in everything you do. Finally, if the unthinkable happens and you are confronted with an abstract topic or topic that you know nothing about, listen to what other people are saying for 3-4 minutes. You will pick up enough hints on things to talk about before jumping into the Group Discussion with your own points.

The Personal Interview is the last stage of your evaluation to get into an IIM, and by far the most important of the factors you can control (the others being your CAT score and the GD), where factors not under your control would include your school and college marks and overall profile.

The Personal Interview (henceforth referred to as PI) offers a golden opportunity to create animpression on your panel which will evaluate you and perhaps deal with you in the future.

Candidates that perform well in the PI despite being average in other areas are sometimes recommended for admission purely on the strength of their interview. On the other hand, there have been cases of candidates who, despite having fantastic profiles, choke under pressure and say something inappropriate which automatically leads to rejection.

There is only one way in which you can do well in the PI, and that is to believe with all your heart that there is an IIM seat with your name written on it, and that you are better than allthe other candidates that have turned up for the interview. This is not arrogance, but belief in you. There will be a hundred factors gnawing at your head before the PI (my GD was poor...my tie is awry...I don't have all the required photocopies...), and the only way to ensure that you do not crumble before the interview panel is to be firm in your self-belief.

At the end of the day, your interview is about yourself. I can (and will) tell you some techniques to help you, but your interview is a very personal thing. There is no standard method to do well on an interview, and you can never know how you have done. I have seen a lot of people coming out with smiling faces that have eventually failed to convert their calls, and many people with long faces who have been pleasantly surprised.

If you can maintain your composure during an interview and justify everything that you have put down on your Candidate Information Form (which will be mailed to you along with your interview call letter andhas to be submitted at the time of your interview), you will sail through the interview. Some basics to help you keep your cool are:

1. Be prepared:

Shine your shoes, adjust your tie-knot, comb your hair and arrange all your certificates in chronological order. Carry photocopies of everything. Don't forget your CAT admit-card or the interview call letter. A well-organised candidate creates a good impression on the panel and ensures that the PI has got off to a good start before the questions even begin. Also, when in doubt, always wear a suit.

2. Treat the panellists as humans:

The people interviewing you are not gods. They are professors whom you will have an opportunity to interact with in a few months' time. Don't assume that they know everything, and that they cannot make mistakes. The panellists often have a shallowknowledge of areas that they question you on but ask questions with tremendous self-confidence. Therefore, it is up to you to not stumble at these points. Explain to themwhat you know about the topic. Often, even the most rudimentary answers contain more information than the person asking the question has with him.

3. Be humble:

At the same time, never underestimate the panel. They have knowledge in depth of several diverse fields, and will definitely surprise you with their lines of questioning.

They have far more experience and knowledge than you, and have interviewed candidates like you by the hundreds, so give them their due respect. By thisexperience, they can size you up pretty quickly, and they don't like someone who thinks he is better than them.

4. Don't give a 'stress' interview:

A 'stress' interview exists only in the mind of the interviewee. If the panel start questioning you aggressively, sit back, smile and take your time answering their questions. They will appreciate your composure, and soon revert to a normal interview format.

5. Know what you have written in your Candidate Information form:

The form is one of the few sources of information that the panel has about you, and they will ask you several questions on it. Be prepared to justify every line of what you have written, and don't just write things down for the 'sake' of doing so. A good candidate who can defend his point of view is almost always preferred to a brilliant candidate with a half-hearted defence.

6. Be honest:

The panel will catch you out easily if you are lying unless you are a pathological liar. Dishonesty creates a very bad impression and will almost certainly lead to rejection. Even if you do manage to hoodwink the panel, will you really be comfortable going to an IIM knowing you don't deserve to be there?

7. Say 'I don't know':

It is okay to not know the answer to something the panel asks you. They don't expect you to know everything, and will purposely keep asking you questions to test the limits of your knowledge. I'm not just talking through my hat here. In the 5 IIM interviews that I have attended (ABCLK), I have said 'I don't know' twice or thrice in every interview. Yet every panel saw enough in me to select me.

8. Speak slowly, look everyone in the eye:

Despite what GD/PI coaches say, avoid looking at all the members of the panel while answering a question. If someone has asked you a question, respect that fact and give him/her your undivided attention while answering. Speaking slowly helps you gather your thoughts and stops you from blurting out incoherent or inappropriate sentences.

9. Be diplomatic:

The IIMs like 'safe' candidates. This is because mavericks rarely make good managers and are often more trouble than they are worth in the corporate world. Diplomacy is a valued virtue in any good manager. Therefore, avoid taking a stand during the interview,especially on controversial issues. If you are forced to take a stand, justify completely why your views are what they are, and always admit that there may be opposing views as well. Finally, never criticize anyone, however deserving they may be of censure.

Sidestep the question by saying something like 'I don't know enough to pass judgement.'

10. Ask questions:

The IIMs want you as much as you want them. When the interview is over, and they indicate that you may ask questions, take the opportunity to ask intelligent questions and figure out if that IIM is right for you. Read up on the IIM you are interviewing for, and never belittle the newer IIMs. The panel will appreciate the effort you have made.

11. Don't time your interview:

A shorter interview just means that you were easier to 'read' for the panel and that they judged you faster than some of the other candidates. The duration of your interview has absolutely no relation to how good or bad the interview was.

Remember to always greet the panel with a smile and thank them for their time when you leave. Politeness will hold you in good stead inside the interview room, and outside it as well.

2

Group Discussion

Discussions of any sort are supposed to help us develop a better perspective on issues by bringing out diverse viewpoints. Whenever we exchange differing views on an issue, we get a clearer picture of the problem and can understand it. The understanding makes us better equipped to deal with the problem. This is precisely the main purpose of a discussion. The dictionary meaning of the word Group Discussion is to talk about a subject in detail. So, group discussion may refer to a communicative situation that allows its participants to express views and opinions and share with other participants. It is a systematic oral exchange of information, views and opinions about a topic, issue, problem or situation among members of a group who share certain common objectives.

G D is essentially an interactive oral process. The group members need to listen to each other and use voice and gesture effectively use clear language and persuasive style.

GD is structured: the exchange of ideas in a GD takes place in a systematic and structured way. Each of the participants gets an opportunity to express his/her views and comments on the views expressed by other members of the group.

GD involves a lot of group dynamics, that is, it involves both - person to person as well as group to group interactions. Every group member has to develop a goal oriented or group-oriented interaction. A participant needs to be aware of needs of other group members and overall objectives of the discussion.

Definition: Group discussion may be defined as – a form of systematic and purposeful oral process characterised by the formal and structured exchange of views on a topic, issue, problem or situation for developing information and understanding essential for decision making or problem solving.

Nowadays Group Discussion is being extensively used along with personal interviews for the final selection of candidates. It plays a main role in selecting the best among the best. Having scored high marks, students who get selected for a higher course or employment are placed on apar - on equal footing - based on their age, qualification and experience. It becomes necessary to conduct further screening for choosing a few among many. It is here, the Group Discussion plays an important part. It helps in choosing the socially suitable candidate among the academically superior achievers. It is one of the best tools to study the behavioural and attitudinal responses of the participants.

Rightly speaking, Group Discussion is more a technique than a conventional test. In fact, it is one of the most important and popular techniques being used in a few personality tests. It is a technique, or a method used for screening candidates as well as testing their potential. It is also designed as a situation test wherein a sample of a candidate's group worthiness and potential as a worker comes out quite explicitly

FEATURES OF GROUP DISCUSSION

1. Group Discussion, as the name itself indicates is a group activity carried out by participating individuals. It is an exchange of ideas among the individuals of a group on a specific topic.
2. It is used as reliable, testing device - mainly as a tool to assess all the candidates in a group at one go -in order to select the best in comparative perspective.
3. Group Discussion is an informal discussion in which participants of the same educational standard discuss a topic of current interest.
4. It is also known as leaderless discussion. It means its aim is to find out the natural leadership level of the candidates. Strictly speaking, no one from the group or outside will be officially designated as leader or president or chairman or anything of the sort. Even the examiner or supervisor who launches the discussion will retire to the background. No one will participate or intervene in the deliberations of the group.

NATURE AND SCOPE

Why you are now being tested after successfully passing out the written examination and perhaps the interview too?

You have successfully completed the written examination which tests the knowledge of different subjects as well other capabilities like writing skill, numerical and cognitive ability, test of reasoning, general knowledge etc., Exactly like you, other participants who have come to the final round of selection after thorough screening are of the same qualification. Their age-group, educational qualifications, academic achievements and background experiences are generally quite similar and all of you are of the same level.It is necessary that you should understand the nature of the G D technique as well as its rationale and purpose. It is very important to know what personality traits the examiners would focus on. If you want to attain success in this challenge test, you should analyse its ingredients and grasp its techniques.

As all the participants in a Group Discussion are rivals, there is bound to be competition and clash of interests among them. Everyone in the group would be keen to top in the discussion, resulting in a good deal of rivalry and manoeuvring for situations of advantage. Thus, in the group discussion- in this free for all- you must manage others and get the cooperation of the group by continuously relating to situations as they keep developing and changing. The dynamics of the group will stimulate each candidate to reveal his/her inherent natural leadership qualities in a spontaneous manner. But only those who remain alert by adapting himself/herself to the changing situations as they emerge, and only those who utilize the opportunities with enterprise, imagination and tact come out successfully.

Under these circumstances, the conduct and behaviour of each candidate will bring to the surface his or her natural leadership, social, dynamic and organizing abilities in a spontaneous manner. Group Discussion is essentially a verbal-oriented performance and you must talk your way out. With one's gift of the gab or power of expression. GD also requires the verbal display of the knowledge of the candidate. The more your ideas and the more your knowledge of the subject, the more interested, enthusiastic and confident you would become and the more fluent and forceful would be your speech and contribution to the discussion.

WHAT IS TESTED IN-GROUP DISCUSSION?

The rationale of the GD technique rests on the principle that leadership qualities with knowledge and power of expression are essential to achieve the results or objectives in all group endeavours. The leadership quality of one can nowhere be more clearly revealed than in a group discussion. For instance, see the difference between GD and other forms of testing.

There is a considerable difference between public speaking and GD. In public speaking, the audience merely judges and passes a verdict on the speaker. Nobody in the audience competes with you. They listen to what the speaker says but do not compete with the speaker. They listen to what the speaker says, but do not discuss the subject with equal rights as does the speaker.

The same is the case with an interview. In an interview, a candidate has to deal with the interviewer who asks questions to which the interviewed responds. He will be given ample opportunities as the interviewer is interested in the answers. In a debate or lecture, the candidate is given some time to think and marshal his ideas and the chairman or the presiding officer will ensure that no one intervenes. The interview focuses on personality traits wherein the interviewers ask well directed questions to assess the overall personality of a candidate.

Yet these tests by themselves are insufficient, as they do not test the group worthiness of a candidate, a quality that is an important component for success in all vocations.

WHAT ARE THE DESIRABLE ATTITUDES IN GD?

The participants should adopt two important attitudes which alone will facilitate a productive and satisfying outcome in any Group Discussion:

1. All participants in the group must accept responsibility for the smooth conduct of the group activities. This orientation means that each member takes on leadership responsibilities even though he is not entrusted any such a role. Instead of passively waiting for someone else to do what must be done, everyone must actively seek and accept responsibility. In an effective group discussion, there are no absolute followers, but different levels and kinds of leaderships and these leaderships keep fluctuating.

2. Another important attitude is open-mindedness -the willingness of the candidate to consider a broad range of ideas and suggestions from others. He must be flexible and must be open to change. Instead of taking rigid stands on issues, the flexible member tries to adapt to the best interests of the group. This requires objectivity- to make unbiased, impartial judgments. This does not mean that you completely suppress your subjective and emotional reactions. You try to balance them with objective observations. This requires maintaining a proper perspective, that is, either becoming too neither involved in problems to maintain objectivity nor remaining too distant and uninvolved to be fully unaware of their nature. Finally, the participant with the orientation of equality should not nourish notions of superiority and must realize that the fellow participants are equal to him/her in all aspects. You also get an opportunity of noticing and comparing the verbal ability, depth of knowledge, extent of ideas, logical reasoning and the convincing capacity of others and this should enable you to prepare yourself to match with them.

3. How to Lead Group Discussions

I. Introduction:

In this sub chapter, we are going to explore how to lead discussion groups. Have you have ever led a discussion group? From your experience, what are the essential ingredients in a good group discussion? Take a moment to think this through and jot some answers down. Now think about the following questions for a while. When would you want to use a group discussion? When would you not want to use it? What are the drawbacks to group discussion? Write your answers before proceeding to the next section.

II. Understanding the Dynamics of a Group Discussion.

A. Good group discussion is impossible without three key ingredients:

1. The leader must be committed to having an open discussion. The group leader has the responsibility of asking the types of questions that will stimulate discussion and draw out each group member. The group leader needs to know the answers, but more importantly, he or she needs to lead the group to discover the answers for themselves.

2. Each group member must contribute in a positive way to the discussion, offering input and encouraging participation by others. A passive or aggressive group member will stifle discussion. Each group member's opinion is valuable to the group. No one should be allowed to dominate the discussion or intimidate the others into silence.
3. The whole group should manifest an environment of acceptance. It should be a "safe" place to express an opinion. The group atmosphere should be one in which no answer or opinion is ridiculed. A wrong answer should be correctly refined and clarified, but not ridiculed, put down and ignored.

B. There are two main elements on which group interaction is based. They are interdependent and together determine the dynamic of the group discussion.
   1. The element of content: The content of the discussion must answer questions and draw conclusions. It must result in application in their lives.
   2. The element of personalities: This includes how easily each member opens up and shares with one another and how skilfully the leader involves the various people.

C. Benefits of group discussion.
   1. It does not require the leader to have public speaking ability to be successful in ministering to people.
   2. Members are more involved in interactive learning than from a passive lecture format.
   3. It increases feedback by providing opportunity for further thought, investigation and personal interaction with the issues discussed. Group discussions are likely to produce people with well-thought-through personal convictions.
   4. It increases leadership and self-confidence in those who participate.

D. Limitations of a group discussion
   1. It requires thorough preparation on the part of the leader. The leader must know the material well enough to respond to a variety of questions from the group.
   2. It is not the place to present a large volume of material. Spending plenty of time in discussion will limit the amount of time devoted to the leader imparting information.

3. It requires preparation by all group members. Preparation is essential to avoid sharing their ignorance and biblically unfounded opinions.
4. There is the danger of "group think". The leader does not take control and allows the group to make the final decision, which may or may not be consistent with the Scriptures.

In what ways is preparation for a discussion group different from preparing for a non-discussion group? How do you prepare for a discussion group? Write down your answers before proceeding to Section III.

III. How to prepare for good group discussion. Good discussion takes work. Here is what to do:

A. Be aware of the needs of your group members. Think through their needs and how the time together can help meet those needs.

B. Study your material and plan your presentation.
   1. Determine your goals—what are you trying to accomplish?
   2. Determine what questions you will use to stimulate extended discussion. Do not ask simple "yes or no" questions, but rather ask those questions that will get group members talking about the how-to's and the why's.
   3. Plan (write out) summary statements and application points you want to communicate during the discussion. This will help avoid "group think." You want your group members to apply the word to their lives, not merely answer questions. At appropriate points in the discussion and at the end of the meeting, you will need to summarize the conclusions reached by the group and apply them to life.

C. Think through possible responses. This will help you be prepared for whatever happens.

D. Go through the study yourself and try it out. Preparation is the key.

IV. How to lead your group effectively.

A. Create a good atmosphere for learning.
   1. Get excited about the Word of God.

2. Get excited about what they are discovering. Remember how excited you were when you learned these things for the first time? Share in their excitement.
3. Use a "hook" (attention-getter) to begin. A good hook helps expose a need; it answers the question: why should we discuss this topic? Examples of "hooks" can be anything from a short motivational story ending with an unsolved question posed to the group, to agree-disagree question or brief two-by-two discussions of a provocative question.
4. Use good questions to generate discussion. Good questions get people thinking. This will be discussed more in section V.
5. Balance the priority of getting through the material with the needs your group members might bring up. Your goal is to relate life-changing material to the lives of the group members, not to merely go through the material regardless of needs.

B. Summarise the lessons learned and draw out appropriate applications. You want your group to apply the content to their lives, not just repeat it back to you. The nature of group discussions often leaves the main ideas and applications unclear. The leader needs to make them clear by summarizing at appropriate times.

C. Make assignments for further study for the next meeting. In order to have them prepare for the next meeting you will need to work through what the group will do at that meeting and make assignments accordingly.
All discussion groups have problems. What are some that you have faced? How have you dealt with them? Write down your answers before proceeding to section D.

D. Deal with the barriers to good discussion.
1. Competing opinions. The best answer to two opinions that disagree is to find God's answer in the Bible. Often you can deal with this by asking "What do the rest of you think?" If you do not know the solution, look it up and bring back the answer the following week.
2. Getting off on tangents. The leader must be the one to get the discussion back on track. Suggest that topics not directly related to the discussion can be discussed after the meeting.

3. Difficult personalities. Some people require more patience, wisdom and tact than others. You can limit the response of aggressive talkers by asking, "What do some of the rest of you think?" Or you could direct a question to someone else. (*for example,* if Mark is answering all the questions before anyone else in the group, say "John [or the name of anyone else in the group], what do you think...?") If a person still tends to dominate, talk to him after the meeting. Dogmatic and opinionated group members, as well as passive, unresponsive members, can stifle a discussion. A good idea is to place aggressive talkers next to you. Consider meeting individually with these group members to discuss how they can best contribute to the group.

Good questions are the fuel for good discussion groups. Those same good questions are the oil that keeps the group moving. What have you learned about asking good questions?

All questions are not alike. In fact, some destroy group discussion. Questions are like tools. We need to match them to the desired outcome. Good discussion requires that the students have a certain body of knowledge. Some questions check knowledge, other questions refine it.

V. How to use good questions.

A. The four types of questions:

1. Questions that have only one obvious answer ("closed" or "leading"). A leading question is one that implies the answer that the leader expects. Examples: "What character quality is Paul speaking of in 1 Corinthians 13?" "Paul was a committed Christian, wasn't he?" The value of a "closed" question is that it uncovers specific details that the students know and reveals to them and to the teacher what they do not know. It narrows the range of the discussion. A leading question that can be helpful is: "Do you all agree with what was said?" This is helpful in correcting a wrong answer because the correction will (hopefully) come from their peers instead of the discussion group leader. Danger: Too many closed questions or leading questions communicate a lack of preparation on the teacher's part and a low view of the students. It can also block discussion.

2. Questions that suggest only a few specific responses ("limiting"). A limiting question limits the learners' thoughts to the specific details or thoughts desired by the leader. Students become frustrated as they unsuccessfully try to read the discussion group leader's mind. Examples: "Who were Paul's two main disciples?" "What one verse in the Bible best summarizes the whole Bible?" The value of a limiting question is that it limits the scope of the discussion. Danger: Like closed questions.
3. Questions that invite personal opinionto have a large number of answers or no obvious answers ("open, wide-open"). An open question allows the group to explore causes, reasons, places, conditions, results, etc., without feeling confined. It does not require a specific number of answers, thus leaving the discussion open to many opinions. Value: It gets to beliefs and values of the students. It helps them develop new possibilities. "Open" questions encourage the group to express their personal opinions and take into consideration the answers of others in the group. This greatly aids the learning process. Examples: "Why do you think Paul disciple people?" "What are some reasons given in this passage?" "What does it really mean to 'disciple' someone?" Danger: With an inaccurate foundation, these questions can lead to wrong conclusions. This can lead to "group-think". 4. Questions from members of the group that the leader asks the group to respond to first ("relay"). A relay question draws the rest of the group into a discussion, after one member answers a question, expresses an opinion, or gives a wrong answer. Example: "You heard what Tom said about discipleship. Now, what do the rest of you think?" Group members are encouraged not only to consider the opinions of others, but also to think for themselves. Danger: If not used properly, these can intimidate or embarrass a quiet person. This, too, can also lead to group-think.

B. Using questions effectively.
   1. Think through the specific point each question is to bring out.

2. Be ready to rephrase or ask additional clarifying questions if members do not understand a question.
3. Do not be afraid of silence. Let the members think through their answers and gain courage to speak.

VI. Application and Close

Think about the last small group you led or participated in. Go to the last page of these notes and analyse the group according to each question. Think about what went well and how things could have been improved. Be prepared to discuss this in class and with your mentor.

Discussion Questions:

1. What are the dynamics of a group discussion?
2. How do you prepare for and lead an effective group discussion?
3. How do you use good questions to stimulate group discussion?

Characteristics of Successful Group Discussion

For any group discussion to be successful, achieving group goal is essential. Following characteristics are necessary:

Having a clear objective -The participants need to know the purpose of group discussion so that they can concentrate during the discussion and contribute to achieving the group goal. An effective GD typically begins with a purpose stated by the initiator.

Motivated Interaction: When there is a good level of motivation among the members, they learn to subordinate the personal interests to the group interest and the discussions are more fruitful.

Logical Presentation: Participants decide how they will organise the presentation of individual views, how an exchange of the views will take place, and how they will reach a group consensus. If the mode of interaction is not decided, few of the members in the group may dominate the discussion and thus will make the entire process meaningless.

Cordial Atmosphere: Development of a cooperative, friendly, and cordial atmosphere avoids the confrontation between the group members.

Effective Communication skills: The success of a GD depends on an effective use of communication techniques. Like any other oral communication, clear pronunciation, simple language, right pitch are the pre-requisites of a GD. Non-verbal communication has to be paid attention to since means like body language convey a lot in any communication.

Participation by all candidates: When all the members participate, the GD becomes effective. Members need to encourage each other in the GD.

Leadership Skills: Qualities like initiation, logical presentation, encouraging all the group members to participate, summarising the discussion reflect the leadership qualities.

Meeting Evaluation Worksheet

As soon as possible after the meeting, evaluate it using the following questions. For the first few times, it will be helpful to make your evaluation in writing.

1. Was everyone at the meeting who should have been there? What needs to be done to contact anyone who was absent?
2. Did you begin and end on time? What is necessary to improve on this?
3. Were you thoroughly prepared for the session? What would enable you to be better prepared for subsequent sessions?
4. What was your goal for this particular session? Was the objective of the session reached in (each member's) life? Why or why not?
5. Did everyone participate in the discussion? Did certain people tend to dominate or be left out of the discussion? What can be done to produce a better balance?
6. Did people open up to share their thoughts, or did you have to carry the discussion? Were you able to draw the correct answers from the group rather than giving them the answers? What could be done to improve this?
7. Did the group get off on unprofitable tangents? How can you better keep the discussion on target?
8. Was the discussion theoretical or was it practical and relative to the lives of the people involved? How could you have better related it to practical Christian living?
9. Did everyone reach the desired conclusions, or did some go away with unresolved questions? Are there people in the group that you should meet with for personal counsel before the next session?

10. What other suggestions can you make that will enable you to do a better job in your next session?

HOW IS THE PERFORMANCE JUDGED?

Selection is done based on the impact created by each candidate on the group. Who does get selected?

- One who expresses his ideas well?
- One who has sound arguments and shows keenness and interest.
- One who has sufficient knowledge of his subject and convinces the group by his argumentative presentation.
- One who has a logical and systematic approach?

Above all, it is the one who has the tendency to cooperate and who does the coordination and is liked by the group.

HOW TO START PARTICIPATING?

Group discussion tasks involve many roles for the participants to take up. Choosing any role, each participant can perform multiple functions. Any discussion starts with an initiative made by one. Someone should propose the subject with his/her ideas or procedures. This gets the group started. Since getting started on any task is usually difficult, this is an important role. Inevitably he/she who do this take up the presiding or leading role. Further he needs to produce new ideas and perspectives for the continued life of a group.

Okay. You missed the opportunity. Someone, a more tactful candidate has taken up the lead role. What is left for you?

There are still ways.

You can furnish more information by usurping his place. You can politely indulge giving evidence, opinions and relate experiences, personal or others, relevant to the discussion. In fact the quality of the discussion is dependent on the information generated out of the discussion. The more information you provide on the subject, the more prominent your place will become in the group.

Okay. You missed this opportunity too. A vociferous participant has stolen the show. All have nothing to do except to listen. The best way is to play the role of an information seeker thereby making your participation important. By way of asking information from others and seeking clarification one can make his participation felt.

There are various ways to make your presence important. Instead of just presenting information one can strongly present his own point of view. Usually people will not reveal their opinions out of fear of criticism. But an effective presenter expresses the opinions freely and is prepared to invite argument to his side. By stating one's own beliefs, attitudes and judgments, one can take up a main position in the discussion. But you must ensure that your opinion is on the winning side and there is nothing negative in your opinion because a negative opinion is disliked by others.

Another role left for you is this: Ifyou cannot make up your position, prevail upon the opinions of others. The effective participant actively seeks other's attitudes and convictions, especially of those members who are hesitant to speak. Unlike others who are content with presenting their own views and neglecting other opinions you will win the favour of other participants by seeking their opinions.

There is always room for participation if you elaborate the ideas of others and clarify as well as expand the opinions of others through relevant examples and explanations. This is the best way to attract the attention of the rest.

Slow and steady, you can win the race. If you have not yet got an opportunity, take up the role ofintegrator who classifies the relationships between various facts, opinions and suggestions and integrates the ideas of others thereby assuming the main role of presenter. After a considerable time has been spent on discussion, the need for integrating and summarizing all that transpired so far becomes essential. You can do that by way of orientation, that is, by keeping the group directed toward its goal, by summarizing what has taken place and clarifying the purpose or position of the group. Essentially you insure that the group has a direction and that it heads in the "right" direction and assumes the role of a leader.

There are some more ways in which the participants can take up group maintenance. You should make your presence important by initiating the group's interpersonal relationships. An encouraging speaker is always liked by fellow participants. He praises and agrees with others providing a warm support to others. But one ought to be careful because he who is a contestant should maintain his position keeping his attention on excelling others. Similarly, your sense will be appreciated if it does relieve tension. It will be very much appreciated as you create a relaxed atmosphere by reducing formality and interjecting humour. When tension increases, people become emotionally involved which will not be conducive for smooth discussion. At times the role of pacifying others and providing relief will achieve leadership position. Equally important is the role of one who controls the channel of communication providing proper balance in the amount of participation of each member. You can also gain the leading position by encouraging those who might otherwise not speak while tackling those who tend to dominate over others or monopolize the discussion

What Are to Be Avoided?

There are certain attitudes which act negatively, and they spoil the chances of selection. Constantly objecting others and speaking pessimistically will block the smooth flow of discussion. A totally negative attitude prevents progress and people who are always complaining and always dissatisfied will not be found suitable. Equally unsuitable are those who insult and criticize others betraying jealousy or animosity. The aggressive attitude is usually disapproved. Another avoidable attitude is telling irrelevant stories and personal experiences. Motivated by a need for attention, some participants interject comments that call attention to their achievements and successes. They are boastful while trying to appear not tobe so.

What is the secret of scoring sure success in a group discussion?

The examiners usually look for a very positive personality with varied potential. During the progress of any group discussion, there will be conflicting views and as a result, heated arguments. The winner has to reveal his positive personality traits and leadership abilities to gain approval for his ideas. Since the test is conducted without a leader, there are opportunities for the individuals who reveal leadership qualities to become group leaders. Seizing the opportunity, the aspirant should impress and influence the group.

The ability to speak is the foremost of all. If one does not speak eloquently and fluently, one cannot create any impact and make his presence strongly felt. One must arouse other's interest by the power of expression. While talking there must be sense. Conveying all information in well-balanced sentences in a manner that reflects a good grasp of the subject will indicate sharp and analytical mind. The delivery should be smooth and catching. Important of all is the tone. It should reflect the humility of a very knowledgeable person. There will be interruptions and they should be borne with patience and a winning smile. It is the ability to hold the attention of group members which matters.

How Can A Topic Be Analyzed?

While speaking on given topic it is necessary to analyse the topic considering its salient aspects and finding out a well-reasoned solution. One must think of sound arguments in support of one's point of view and a logical presentation of them. It is necessary to consider the pros and cons of the given problem. Use of available information including those of others is important. Synthesizing different points of view and answering them in such a way as supportive of one's case is talent which must be cultivated. Considering an issue or a problem in a broader angle putting the immediate concerns in broader issues, thereby displaying the extent of knowledge is a successful technique. But one ought to be careful without becoming irrelevant or boastful.

Avoiding any repetition of ideas or arguments is important. Keeping within the scope of the given subject one must contribute towards rising the intellectual level of the discussion.

How to Excel Others ina Group?

A good support always results in a good relationship with others, which eventually brings success. Rapport building starts from the very first step. But there must be conflicting opinions which alone will help to look at a problem from various angles and come up with alternatives. As such when conflicting viewpoints arise, they should be resolved by active participation and a positive attitude. One can certainly disagree giving sound and valid reasons for disagreement but one's behaviour should not be disagreeable. One's pleasantries, attitude of cooperation and sharing experiences with others, expressing compliments and gratitude on what others say-all create an attraction towards oneself. Maintaining mutual respect will avoid critical judgment of others. One's efforts at preventing the proceedings from going astray, encouraging non-participants to enter the discussion and tactful handling of conflicting opinions with a view to bringing about consensus will win the admiration of other members of the group. Another important reason of success is being attentive to others' point of views and analysing them in alogical manner even for disagreeing.

REASONS FOR SELECTION: A FEW COMMENTS

No.1 (Comments at two stages of one's participation)

Beginning: No1 has displayed excellent leadership ability and handled an explosive situation with tact and understanding. He has found an acceptable and workable solution by displaying excellent resourcefulness. He avoided an open split and confrontation by voluntarily surrendering the privilege of being got elected as chairman by majority vote. Thus, he has given greater importance to group needs than for his own selfish requirements. He also won 7 by persuasion and by personal example.

Ending: A brilliant and outstanding exposition is presented by No.1 in admirable and extremely convincing manner. His approach is objective and balanced. This candidate, who had displayed consistently remarkable leadership qualities and coordinating ability earlier, now reveals intellectual maturity, balanced judgement and excellent power of persuasion. Socially he is well adjusted and has the resourcefulness to cope with difficult individuals and situations. To sum up, he is an outstanding candidate with high level of leadership qualities. He is specially commended and selected with top rating.

No.3 is an intelligent, imaginative and dynamic leader. His approach has throughout been positive and constructive He is also able to get along well and harmoniously with all. He can judge and assess others correctly and wins over everyone with tact and understanding. His enterprising attitude, keenness to shoulder responsibility and capacity to compromise successfully with crisis and obstacles enable him to establish himself as the natural leader. In this group he is the outstanding coordinator and leader. He is selected with top grading No.3 has grasped the subject very well and explained its scope very lucidly. Hehas gone about his task with a purpose, plan and system, revealing organization and method. He spoke to the point and made a strong impact on the group. He is decisive, enterprising and takes reasonable risks. We saw that he took a prominent part during the early stages and made useful contribution. He has good material and selected with high grading.

No.4 has readily and cheerfully accepted the responsibility and made good use of the opportunity given to him. He has consistently been displaying initiative, drive, enterprise and imagination. Now he has known excellent grasp of the subject and explained facts of a sensitive nature in an easy and effortless manner. He has created a very strong and favourable impact on the group with his conduct, ideas and example. As was shown by No.3, the group is eager to hear him further. But as a disciplined organiser and planner, No.4 wants the discussion to proceed asdecided earlier. He is more team oriented and keen to promote group activity. His approach is positive and contribution constructive. He has displayed high degree of leadership throughout. It is selected with high rank rating.

No.7-displayed initiative, urge and drive and shouldered full responsibility to launch the group on its objective. He is gifted in all spheres-intellectual, organisational, dynamic and social. He has extensive knowledge. He has pressed his case from a new angle and succeeded fully in carrying the audience with him. He is bold and faces the challenge with courage and determination, intelligence and imagination. Selected and accorded top rating.

Reasons for Rejection

The keenness and eagerness of No.3, his readiness to shoulder responsibility, his confidence to face the group and his initiative are no doubt his plus points. But his approach is selfish, authoritarian and annoying to others. He is too assertive and very dominating. His brazen attempt to bulldoze others will provoke them and result in quarrels and clashes. These, in turn, will hinder group activity and realisation of the common goal objective, which is successful completion of the discussion within the time allotted. A leader or manager must carry his teammates with them and not antagonize them. No.3, unfortunately, appears to be lacking in this very important aspect. REJECTED

No.2 He does not know much about the subject and he has the gift of the gab and hence waffles aimlessly. There is no logic or rationale in what he said he lacks organisation, system and order. He talks at random, jumping from one topic to another in fits and starts. Earlier we saw him acting rigidly and selfishly. He will cause friction and quarrels in the team, behaving like a bull in china shop. REJECTED

No.5 had remained aloof and silent throughout. He is dull and devoid of ideas. He admits his limitations but does not show any interest or determination to overcome them. He wastes opportunities and shies away from responsibility. Being weak and docile and unenterprising, he will not be able to come up as a leader. REJECTED

No.8 this candidate is a mere camp follower without any initiative, urge, drive or originality. He finds excuses to avoid and shirk responsibility. He has throughout been disinterested, distant and aloof and has not made any contribution to group activity. An extremely dull and insipid individual will prove to be a great burden to the organization. REJECTED

No.1 wastes the opportunity offered to him on a platter. On his own also he did not display and initiative and drive. He pleads ignorance and confirms that he lacks ideas. This is a general knowledge topic and anyone familiar with current events should be able to make some interesting contribution to the discussion. He offers excuses and prefers to be the last speaker. If he does not know, he can at least ask a knowledgeable colleague in the group to explain the nature and scope of the topic first. On the other hand, he straightway shirks responsibility. He is a dull and insipid candidate who lacks self-confidence and leadership potential. REJECTED

Sulks and refuses to cooperate. He also wastes the good opportunity offered to him. He is rigid and fails to adapt himself to the situation. He has good expressive faculty, but his ideas are confused and overlapping. He waffles unnecessarily instead of going directly to the point. His ego and pride prevent him from extending cooperation and establishing rapport. Because of his personal quarrel with No.6, he refuses to the half of the group. With this marked negative qualities. No.2 will be a serious hindrance to the team. REJECTED

This candidate has understood the subject and has the self-confidence to the challenge No.5 and produces quite a few original and convincing arguments to support his stand. But he continues his collision path. He prefers to attack those who disagree with him in a brutal and direct manner. He quarrelled with No.2 violently earlier. Now he repeats the same behaviour pattern. It is doubtful whether he could improve by training. REJECTED

This candidate lacks initiative and originality. His ideas are limited he has nothing useful to contribute. He is afraid to take any firm decision and commit himself. He has wasted the opportunity afforded to him. With such marked negative qualities he cannot make the grade as a strong leader. REJECTED

Aactive and well- motivated group in which No.7 and 5 display natural leadership qualities and prove successful in launching the group on its task. They overcome the obstacles which they encounter with imagination, speed and tact. This GD being a team work, it cannot be executed without someone assuming the responsibilities of a leader and coordinator. Nos. 1, 2 and 3, though spoke among themselves, did not come toward to shoulder this responsibility on their own initiative. On the other hand, No.7 displayed natural leadership abilities and assumed the responsibility to launch the group on its task, on his own No.5 who gave excellent support to No.7, also displays good leadership qualities. We find No.2 to be hesitant, diffident and overcautious. No.1 appears to be lacking in ideas and he is unable to half No.2 actively. Without admitting his limitations No.1 tries to evade the issues or pass the buck on the others. No3has acted in light vein which indicates certain amount of irresponsibility Nevertheless he offers to be the opening speaker. Hence, he has to be watched further, Nos.4, 6and 8 have so far remained as silent spectators.

In this group Nos.3 and 7 initially wanted to assume leadership and made their debuts. But they bitterly quarrelled between themselves as to who should be the leader. Unfortunately, both lacked tact and social co-hesiveness. They were also rigid and selfish. Team spirit and cooperation on the part of both were sadly lacking and they were obstructing the progress of group activity. On the other hand, No.1 emerged as the natural and highly gifted leader. He was able to motivate his team mates and move the group towards its goal with remarkable success. He could handle Nos.3and 7 with competence and else displaying appropriate techniques. Nos.5 and 4 came forward to lend good support to No.1 and showed adequate leadership traits themselves No.6,8 and 2 were ineffective camp followers and did not make any contribution to promote group activity. Thus, the only successful candidates of this group are Nos.1, 5 and 4 in that order.

DISCUSSION PAPER

Your Discussion Paper should consist of 4 sections, each approximately one half page of single spaced text. You need to write 3 Papers in all; due the day of the Class Discussion (no late exceptions will be granted). These are in addition to your Poster presentation, meaning that you cannot submit a report on the paper you are presenting. If you wrote a genome project proposal, it will substitute for one of these Discussion Papers. If you choose to do more than 3 Papers, I will give you the grade for the 3 best ones you write.

Section 1: Write a succinct one paragraph summary of the objectives and conclusions of the paper. A good summary is quantitative where appropriate (don't write "they saw some differences in some of the genes", rather write "5,702 of the 17,680 genes on the array were found to be significantly differentially expressed"). Also try to give a little bit of background to why they performed the study, but remember that you are writing scientifically, not for a magazine. Writing should be sharp and to the point, not poetic and superficial.

Section 2: Describe the work flow of the paper. You might even consider drawing out a flow diagram to help you but convert this into text for your paper. This section should be more than a list of the experiments they performed: try to portray the logical connection between the experiments. For example, the authors start by doing X, which leads them to suspect Y, so they did Z, which implied A and led them to conclude C. This should help you to see the logic of the approach, and if you see a flaw in the logic or feel that the conclusions are unjustified, explain why you think that is the case.

Section 3: Highlight the strengths and weaknesses of the paper. You ought to be able to pinpoint three of each. Strengths might be that the study developed a new technology, or led to a new model of some process, or was a particularly clever design. Weaknesses might be that the sample size was too small, orthat the experiment was misinterpreted, or that the study was poorly designed. You should ask yourself whether the paper achieved the objective the authors set themselves. Try to avoid complaining that you did not understand the paper because it was full of jargon or the statistics were too hard for you to follow: I expect that will often be the case, but usually it is because it is assumed that the papers are written for experts. If you have something you don't understand, email or ask me.

Section 4: Think of two experiments that you would propose to follow-up on the paper. Don't just write down the experiments, explain why you would do them and briefly outline what the procedure would be so that they make scientific sense. I expect that you may come up with some crazy ideas, and that some of the experiments will not be feasible. That is OK – I know you don't know enough to be certain about things. In this section just be creative and insightful!

3

Group Discussion Preparation and 1001 Questions

1. "If you can dream it, you can do it"

Number of members= 5 **Time duration= 25 minutes**

A– Every great journey begins with one small step. Similarly, every great success begins with a dream. A dream is what it takes to make things happen in our unique world. Dreams hitch our wagons to stars and make us reach for success and prosperity. A person who has no dreams is incapable of living a wholesome, rewarding life.

B– However, it is important to note that to transform our dreams into reality; we must wake up and chase our dreams. We must not dream of acting when the circumstances are ripe or perfect, instead, we must create those circumstances for ourselves because success will never be served to us on a platter. We need to work hard daily and progressively in the direction of achieving our dreams. It is a gradual, continual process. Success cannot be achieved in one fell swoop. It requires patience and perseverance.

C– Dreams are what give meaning to human life. Each day when we wake up and pursue a positive action plan, our life automatically becomes worth living. All great success stories in the world have begun with simple dreams, executed by utmost care and dedication. For instance, had the Wright brothers never dreamt of a flying machine, we would have never had the luxury of covering great distances across the globe in a matter of hours. As a result, we would have remained in our own comfortable little shells, not knowing about the wonders which awaited us in far off and distant lands.

D– Dreamers are often labelled as wastrels by our society, since they are, ostensibly, not performing any perceivably productive task. Such is the height of our utilitarianism and emphasis on reason and logic, as dreams are dismissed as a waste of time and effort because nothing comes of dreaming, in the stereotypical conviction. The people who actually do? something are not dreamers, they are men of action, who fill each second of their lives with positive action and result-oriented performance. Dreamers are looked down upon as lesser beings, which have nothing constructive to do. They are often dismissed as day- dreamers who engage in useless pursuits because they have nothing else to do. It is essential to understand that it all begins with a dream – no matter how far-fetched or unachievable a task might seem, what the human mind conceives it achieves. And therein lies the beauty of life.

E– One must work towards making one's dreams come true. At the end of each day, it is important to introspect and ask oneself – how much further has one proceeded towards achieving one's dream? What other efforts need to be made? How can one enhance one's quality of life? Trying to discover answers to all such questions will inculcate within us a habit of continual dedication. We will become better human beings, as we will begin to have a sense of purpose and duty.

CONCLUSION– Dreams are the stepping stones upon which the foundations of our lives are laid. More essential than conceiving a dream is to pursue it whole-heartedly even in the face of dire adversity. Mere dreaming has not led anyone anywhere. Implementation of a proper strategy will ensure fulfilment of dreams and a fuller, vibrant life.

2. "Employability skills can't be learned overnight"

Number of participants: 10 **Time:30 Minutes**

A– The employment scenario in the contemporary world is dismal. Today our youth are accumulating degrees by the dozen but they lack the necessary 'employability' skills which can land them respectable jobs corresponding to their level of educational qualification and subject-matter expertise.

B– Of course employability skills are a must in this world of cut-throat competition where the next individual is always more well-qualified and well-prepared. One cannot afford to neglect this skill-set especially in the era of globalization, in the inter-connected nature of the present-day world.

C– Today, youths across nations compete against each other to get that 'best' job. Employability skills are those skills necessary for getting, keeping and being successful in a job. They are the skills and attitudes that enable employees to get along with their colleagues, to make critical decisions, solve problems, develop respect and ultimately become strong ambassadors for the organisation.

D– Employability or ,,soft skills? are the foundations of our career. They are the building blocks. Several graduate and post-graduate students, although masters in their respective fields, lack these skills and hence, end up faring badly in the job market.

E– Several organisations spend a lot of time and money in providing the necessary soft-skill training to their staff, in order to ensure a higher and quality productivity in their employees.

F– Employability skills such as negotiation, decision-making, problem solving, communication skills, critical thinking skills, assertiveness, personal presentation, delegation and so on are the life blood of any organisation. Thus, it is imperative to gain knowledge of them over a sustained period and call them into action when required

G– These skills are not acquired overnight. It is a gradual process which occurs by reading books on personality development, communication skills, listening to motivational tapes and putting their teachings to practise at the requisite moment.

H– The essential employability skills can be divided into - foundational, interpersonal and communication skills - such as being dependable, friendly, polite, adaptability, constructive criticism, task completion, listening, understanding, respect for co-workers and so on.

I– Other employability skills are - problem solving, conflict resolution, critical thinking, and honesty, contribution to team goals, honesty and professionalism. It is believed that the current supply of graduates is broadly acceptable in terms of quantity; there are question marks over quality – especially what they're studying and how they use what they've learnt. Thus, employability skills are highly valued.

J– There is no single, unitary method to learn employability skills - they must be central to one's education. They must be embedded within education programmes, and not treated as marginal, so that their practical application can be ensured. Conclusion Employability skills need patience and perseverance to be perfected. They cannot be mugged up or learnt by heart overnight. They should be developed and tested continuously.

3. "MBA means assurance of Job" For the Motion

- Undoubtedly, the need for the managers has grown over time and corporate have preferred MBA?s for these positions.
- Various researches suggest that as competition intensifies in an industry, marketing and analytics activity increases, resulting in more demand for MBAs.
- As MNCs expand into emerging markets like India, the demand for MBAs is going to go up.
- Higher GDP growth of emerging nations led by industry has created a platform where skills and knowledge with right attitude are in huge demand.

Professional B-schools have catered to this demand by polishing graduates into world - class professionals. Conclusion Industry will continue to have huge demand for professionals who can take their business forward in an environment of cut-throat competition. B-schools are ready to accept this challenge of developing effective and purposeful managers for the industry. If these two things continue to complement each other, jobs are assured. Against the Motion

- Entry barriers in the education industry have come down drastically, resulting in mushrooming of many new B-schools in the country
- But in this process of expansion, quality of academics has gone for a toss. Moreover, the number of faculty has not increased at the same pace. There is a shortage of quality faculty across the board.
- Moreover, the supply of MBAs has outpaced the demand by the industry. This has made placements very challenging.
- Jobs per se is not an issue, the challenge is to get a job which matches one's expectations from the point of view of profile as well as decent compensation.
- In this scenario, only the best with the right skills and attitude will get quality jobs. Conclusion Just getting into a B-school is not an end. The real challenge starts after that. What a

student does in two years will decide his or her fate? Getting the best out of the B-school should be the real motive of the student. If he does well in that, a good job will automatically be the natural outcome.

4. "Success is a science; if you have the conditions, you get the result" For the Motion

- Success is defined as the accomplishments of a person. It is an event that fulfils the indented purpose in his life. The meaning of success differs from person to person. It is extremely complex as every individual defines it in his own way. For some success means attainment of wealth while for others it is the achievement of his goals.
- Success can be considered a science. If you have set some conditions, you will surely get the result. As science refers to the body of knowledge, success depends upon your knowledge, ability and skills to achieve your desired goals. This knowledge should be sensibly explained and constantly applied and if you have set the targets of success in your mind, no one can stop you from accomplishing your set goals and desired success in whatever form you expect.
- Though achievement of set goals can make you successful for the time being, but it is temporary. Once there is attainment of set goals you proceed for getting more. It is an ongoing process and is tentative in nature. Success is non-dogmatic in nature. There is always much more requirement of what you currently possess. Like science there is always innovation of new goals and aims which need to be realized to be at the top of the world. Conclusion Success has its own definition. People think that the situations and circumstances they possess coerce them to take every next step leading to the ultimate success. Against the Motion
- Success is not a science. There is not any necessity of conditions and situations which drives you to take actions and success. Science involves knowledge and skills to be applied but if you are smart you can be successful. Not only does your intelligence is the primary thing to gain success, you smartness in your every footstep can lead

you miles away you had thought. Similarly, many people don't have any conditions or situations to proceed in their life with such targets; it is their own will which forces them to achieve what they want.

- Success is an inner feeling for self-actualized people. There are no conditions set for them to drive them to success. If they must achieve it they will without considering any circumstances, and in the worst situations also they are focused to their plans. Conclusion People are just concerned with the achievements in their life, no matter what conditions and situations they may have to face in future. They are concentrated and focused on their goals and decisively attain success. They are dedicated to achieve success facing out every problem and hindrances in their path.

5. "You won't get success with Ifs & Buts in life"

Ifs & Buts in your attitude can be a barrier in the path to success. People having an attitude with Ifs and Buts in their life are mostly unsuccessful as they do not welcome everything in life without these two words. So what is the main reason for that? Experience matters a lot in life. There are some people who involve themselves with others in gaining experience. Interacting with others and sharing your views with others is a great way to gain knowledge. Knowledge is something that never goes waste. So, the people who welcome everything happily without arguing are the ones successful in life. On the other hand, the people who always try to block themselves from various opportunities by using various Ifs and Buts often loose themselves from going ahead in life. Without proper experience, no one can reach to the path of success. Without experience, the people often stop themselves from the foundation of success. Ifs and Buts in your mind can make you unsuccessful in life. Usually they do not do the things which they can do. So, it is better that people should move on to something more positive, rather than stopping themselves from various opportunities. The people should try to gain more and more experience and try to share the knowledge to achieve success. The people who restrain themselves from opportunities that come their way are often known as unsuccessful people. And till the time, they realize the fact that they are losing their potential in everything and they are not able to gain success in anything, they have lost everything. The inactivity of them leads to an unsuccessful life.

The people should always try to replace the failure with success by replacing "If" and "But" from their life. This way they can achieve the most from their life without much pain which otherwise will be the barrier in the path to success. The people should look for opportunities everywhere by involving themselves with others and sharing each other's experience. So, if you want to achieve success in your life, then you should positively look for opportunities and also remove the possibility of Ifs and Buts from your life. Then success will automatically come at your door, thus leading to a successful career in your whole life. So start replacing your Ifs and Buts with some positive thoughts.

6. "Money alone can't be motivator"

We have been told from childhood to follow our dreams and not get perturbed by the amount of money we make in the initial stages of our careers. It is true that money alone cannot be a motivator. The amount of money we get for the work we do fluctuates all the time – sometimes, when there is recession, we have to take a pay cut, and when the economy is doing well, we may get a raise. However, that should not determine the amount of hard work we put into our work. We should be driven by our passion and determination to excel in life – only then will we be able to overcome all challenges and succeed in what we do. Life is not a bed of roses – there are ups and downs. There are many obstacles along the way and we may have to struggle at times to overcome these obstacles. Successful people are those who look beyond these obstacles and focus on their goal(s), and they don't get distracted or carried away by money or other gains. Bill Gates and Narayana Murthy did not give up when their businesses did not do well – they learnt from their mistakes and worked hard at achieving their goals. Before setting up Microsoft, Bill Gates had established a company called Traf-O-Data to read raw data from roadway traffic counters and then create reports for traffic engineers. The company was not a roaring success but the experience that Bill Gates got from establishing Traf-O-Data was helpful in setting up Microsoft. If money alone had been the motivator for Bill Gates, we would not have a company called Microsoft today. Money is important for survival, but it should not dictate our lives. Once money starts controlling us, we lose our purpose in life and life becomes meaningless and shallow. A person's success is not measured by how much he/she earns but how much he/she contributes to society. Money is an additional benefit that comes with success. Once we keep this mantra at the back of our heads, we will view success and failure in the same light and we won't get affected by money or the lack of money. In conclusion, money alone cannot be a motivator – if we take steps in life while keeping money at the forefront of our decisions, we will not go far in life. We ought to remember that one can be successful if he is determined in life. He must be focused on his goals and overcome all obstacles and challenges that life throws at him. Only then will he reach his fullpotential. So, don't give up on your dreams – follow your passion and you will reach your destination.

7. "Social networking sites are waste of time for career-oriented youth?"

Members-8 Time-30 minutes in today's era when people don't seem to have time to connect with near and dear ones over a cup of coffee, social networking sites seem to be the perfect solution. The rise and rise of social networking sites in the last decade has come as a saviour for those who cannot and do not want to make the effort of meeting people personally and for those who are always 'busy.'

A. Social networking sites have come as a boon for people wanting to connect with friends, especially old friends with whom they have lost touch. If they can renew their acquaintance just by logging on to one such site, then the emergence of these sites needs to be appreciated.

B. True. Social networking sites have changed the way we communicate with people. It is, now, possible to catch up with old acquaintances as well as make your friends a part of your life by sharing pictures, videos, places you visit and so on.

C. These sites intrude your personal space. By feeling a compulsion to share your personal pictures, videos, location, you are living for others and vying for their approval. Looking for others' approval is a sign of insecurity and lack of confidence.

D. The biggest disadvantage of social networking sites is that one ends up wasting a lot of time. Since, it is addictive in nature, a person surfing these sites loses track of time and ends up wasting quality time that may have been used in some productive activity.

E. This is especially true for career-oriented youth, who desire success and a great career. Due to these sites, they end up spending a lot of their time doing various unproductive activities, time which could have easily been spent in thinking about their careers and improving their performance at work.

F. These sites, at best, serve as mere distractions. The youth of the country, who should be burning the midnight oil to think of becoming productive and successful citizens, instead, focus on keeping up with the latest trends on social networking sites.

G. These sites also become an alternate world for the youth, who find an escape from the drudgery of the real world in the time they spend on such sites. For such people, because they are not able to come to terms with their immediate world, the virtual world becomes a preferred reality.

H. The fact that such sites allow revisiting old ties and acquaintances and keeping in touch does not mean that the nature of interaction and conversation is necessarily qualitative. A major drawback of these sites, especially for the youth, most often than not, they do not gain anything out of it. The quality of conversation, in general, is poor, with the nonsensical gibberish forming a chunk of the talk rather than some meaningful dialogue, which raises the intellect and curiosity of the people involved. Thus, the youth of the country should realize the futility of significant man- hours lost and the futility of spending time on social networking sites. 8. "Hard work or Smart work" Gone are the days when only hard work could get you somewhere in life – today, employers are looking for people who work diligently, in a smart manner. Hard work may help you to complete your tasks, but you may not be able to do so efficiently, and that's where smart work comes into play. When someone works in a smart manner, he not only completes his tasks but ensures that time is utilized properly. A smart worker makes a list of the tasks he needs to do and prioritizes them based on the importance – as such, he completes urgent and important tasks first and leaves the rest for a later date. This way, he does not get bogged down by the enormity of the tasks. In school, we would have come across both hard workers and smart workers – hard workers would study the entire year, make notes and prepare diligently for examinations whereas smart workers would pay more attention to theories or concepts they are unsure of and focus more on these areas and this way, they would work on their weaknesses and ace their examinations. Sometimes, we may see smart workers getting better grades than hard workers and this is because smart workers know how to prioritize their work and manage their time efficiently. Many students have the misconception that the more number of hours they put into their studies the better grades they will get. This is not true. Even if you put in less number of hours into your studies but you manage to grasp the concepts, you will be able to ace the exams too. At work, we come across hard workers, who only focus on getting their work done, but sadly, they don't get the proper recognition from their bosses. This is because they forget to do important things like building good relationships and making their voices heard. In meetings, you should voice out your opinions and during lunch time, you should try to mingle with people so that you stay in their good books. At the time of promotion, it is not the person who puts in the most number of hours who gets promoted but it is the person who has managed to do work on time, taken the time to build relationships with his colleagues and bosses and gone the extra mile to assist his peers. It is not wrong to be a hard worker – hard work is important, no doubt, but it is more important to work smart. So, do not simply focus on your work but get to know people too – try to enhance your interpersonal skills and time management skills and you will get recognition quickly.

8. "If you are aggressive, you will be a winner"

Studies have shown that winners are more aggressive than losers. Be it in a sports competition, in the workplace or at school, people who want to succeed in life will go the extra mile to ensure that they are not defeated. Winners practice hard and are always in a fighting mood. Since winning is their goal, they put their best foot forward to gain success in their lives. Many people associate aggression with negative actions. When one is aggressive, it does not mean that he is going to harm someone. Aggression is a state of mind where one appears calm on the outside but inside, he has a burning desire to attempt a difficult task and succeed in it. David Ortiz, a famous American baseball player, once said, "I try to be as quiet as I can at the plate, but still aggressive". Before India became independent, Mahatma Gandhi fought aggressively for the country. Although he appeared calm on the outside, he was a brave fighter. He did not give up his mission. Without weapons, he fought courageously until India was declared independent. If Mahatma Gandhi had given up during his mission, he would never have been considered a hero and a winner. On the other hand, winners need to possess other qualities apart from aggression. The determination to win should be present in a winner. However, apart from determination, hard work and humility are also required. Many winners tend to be aggressive and arrogant. When one is on a winning streak, he gains confidence. When he becomes over confident, he becomes arrogant and this is the cause of downfall of many bright individuals. Certain roles in the society require one to be aggressive. For example, a salesman must be aggressive in order to make a living. If he is not confident about the product that he is selling, then how can he expect potential consumers to purchase it? The world has become a competitive place for people from all walks of life, including students, employees and sportsmen. To stay ahead in the competition, it is important to stay confident and not get carried away by negative thoughts. Aggression is not linked to violence. When someone is aggressive, he is determined to make it big in life. Determination, coupled with hard work, will help one reach the peak of success. It is true that one should be aggressive in order to be a winner. However, it is important to note that there are many people who may be better that you. So, to remain a winner, it is important to practice humility. 10. "We have lost empathy towards old citizens" Today's world is driven by commercialization, where people are becoming more and more self-centred. There is no time left in people's schedules for empathy, care and concern. In addition, with an increasing number of Indians shifting to foreign lands, there has been a phenomenon of growing distance (both physical and emotional) between the younger and the older generations.

There is no empathy left in the hearts of children today towards old citizens because families have become more nuclear in nature.

In the past, joint families used to exist, which led to people of different generations living under one roof, with the cultivation of social values. In a fast-paced lifestyle that we lead today, it has become difficult to manage time between work and family. And there are no strong bonds between families today, which are why we see the lack of empathy towards old citizens. When travelling in buses or intra-city trains, we do not give up our seats for the elderly. We have become more concerned about our welfare, safety and comfort that we have stopped considering the welfare of others. Old citizens are a burden to the younger population. Today, we see old citizens staying alone or in nursing homes because their children do not have the time for them. We are unable to feel the pain and suffering they go through and keep their emotions at bay. The younger generation has become materialistic, only thinking about physical gains and entertainment. We often forget the hardship our parents had to endure to bring us up, and we take their existence, love and support for granted. In Bangalore, the International Day of Older Persons is celebrated every year on October 1 to cultivate empathy, love and concern towards the older generation. The SSMRV College in Bangalore actively participates in bridging the gap between the older and younger generations, and this is what the entire nation should follow. In fact, we should show love for older citizens all year round instead of compressing all the love into one day – 1st October. The 21st century has seen a shift in importance from intangible goods to tangible goods. Now, it is time to show gratitude to the older generation by setting aside some of our valuable time for their happiness. We ought to remember that we wouldn't be who we are without their support. So, the least we can do as a gesture of gratitude is to show empathy towards them.

1001 Questions for All Occasions

It is better to know some of the questions than all the answers.

—James Thurber

Always we face some difficulties in answering some questions and try to become a master of answering all questions but we unable to answer all questions rapidly. So we must know some questions which are appropriate for all occasions. Following are 1001 questions which are being asked selectively on some point of time: -

The Power of Questions

Questions are great conversation starters. It seems everyone has a story to tell or an opinion to share. And to get it, you need only to ask. Good questions invite people to open about themselves and divulge their thoughts and feelings on a wide variety of topics. They're the secret behind getting acquainted with someone you have recently met or learned something completely new about someone you've known for years. If you learn to pose the right questions, you'll gain a better understanding of who your friends are and what makes them tick.

Don't you appreciate it when someone asks you sincere questions? It conveys an interest in your opinions and insights. It demonstrates a desire to know who you are and what you really think. And that means a lot. There is something powerful about questions that force you to think, look within yourself, examine your heart, and search for answers. And it's in the process of responding to those questions that you often make discoveries about yourself—things you never even realized before. Questions also function remarkably well in the context of discussion groups. They draw group participants into the dialogue—less outspoken individuals are coaxed out of their shells and more talkative types have reigned into focus on the issue at hand. Asking great questions in a group setting is the quickest and easiest way to spark stimulating discussions.

But even though most of us realize the importance of raising questions, asking good ones is sometimes another matter. They are not always that simple to think up. That's where The Complete Book of Questions comes in! This book is one big compilation of questions—1001 questions you can use in just about any context to launch great conversations. And many of these questions are likely to trigger other questions you may also wish to discuss. Think of this book as a tool to spark interaction—to know and understand others, and yourself, better.

All the questions in this book have been divided into ten categories for easy reference. Some questions, of course, might readily fit into multiple categories, so this is just one way to sort them. The box below gives a short description of each category of questions:

Questions	Category	Description
1–100:	Light & Easy	Simple, light-hearted topics
101–200:	Personal Profile	Personality traits and behaviours
201–300:	Preferences	Likes and dislikes, favourites
301–400:	Blast from the Past	Past personal experiences
401–500:	Just Imagine	Speculation and imagination
501–600:	Viewpoints	Opinions and perspectives
601-700:	Hard-Hitting	Deep and challenging themes
701–800:	From the Heart	Feelings and emotions
801–900:	Spiritually Speaking	Basic spiritual subjects
901–1001:	Extreme Spiritual	Matters Complex spiritual issues

INTRODUCTION

Guidelines

Since this is a chapter full of questions, no answers are provided. That's where you and your friends and family members step in! As you use these questions to interact with one another, remember there are no right or wrong answers. Don't feel pressured to respond in any certain way—just be yourself and be true to whom you are. Here are a few additional guide-lines to keep in mind:

- Most of the questions are "open-ended" (seeking expanded responses), while others are "closed-ended" (calling for short, one-word answers). In either case, develop your answer as little or as much as you feel comfortable doing.
- In the rare case you find a question that is irrelevant or not something you wish to answer, simply skip it and pick another one.
- The first several categories of questions are the most non-threatening and, therefore, the easiest to answer. These are the best ones to use with new acquaintances.
- The last few categories contain questions of a deeper nature, which may best be utilized in settings where you know the other participants well and are ready to tackle issues of greater significance.

- The Spiritually Speaking category lists questions that address very basic spiritual issues, while the Extreme Spiritual Matters section includes questions that will stretch and challenge you on your personal spiritual journey.

Applications

There are probably as many ways to put this book to use as there are questions within it! So be creative. Experiment with a variety of methods to apply these questions in different contexts. To get you started, consider the following ideas:

- Whether you're with one other individual or a whole group of people, use this book to spark conversations in different settings and occasions: social and holiday gatherings, road trips, meals, dates, discussion groups, family times, vacations, etc.
- Randomly select a number, read that question, and answer it. Take turns, inviting each person to pick a different number—or, if someone prefers, let him or her answer a question that was previously chosen.
- Limit the questions to be selected to one specific category—or two or three categories. Or open up the options to include each and every question in the book.
- Predetermine one question—or several of them—you'd like everyone in your group to answer.
- If you're in a discussion group, look for relevant questions to use as icebreakers and to supplement your topic of discussion.

Listen Well

Finally, as important as good questions are, nothing compares to the significance of developing the skill of effectively listening to one another. Can you think of a time when a person turned to face you squarely and displayed a sincere desire to fully hear and understand you? Chances are that kind of undivided attention made quite an impact on you. Even though it might be tempting to think instead about how you would respond to a given question, do your best to listen well enough to really understand each other.

As you explore these 1001 questions, make the most of the conversations that ensue. Share your responses openly and listen intently to one another. In so doing, you'll express unselfish candour and respect, which will go a long way toward taking your relationships to a whole new level. Now that's a gift you can treasure!

LIGHT & EASY QUESTIONS

1. Do you squeeze the toothpaste tube or roll it? What's the advantage of your method?
2. How many siblings do you have? What's your birth order?
3. What's something you've won and how did you win it?
4. What's one of your nicknames? What do you prefer to be called?
5. What's something your parents used to say to you as a child that you promised yourself you'd never say—but now you catch yourself saying all the time?
6. What's something you intended to do today, but didn't? Why not?
7. Using only one word per person, what was your first impression of each person present with you now?
8. What's something that people do in traffic that really bothers you?
9. Who is the closest friend you've ever had? Describe that relationship.
10. What books on your shelf are begging to be read?
11. What room in your house best reflects your personality? Explain why.
12. How often do you doodle? What do your doodles usually look like?
13. What do you do if you can't sleep at night? Do you count sheep, toss and turn, or get up and try to do something productive?
14. Which do you do more often: hum or whistle? Hum or whistle your answer.
15. What animal are you the most like? Why?
16. How many days could you last in solitary confinement? How would you do it?
17. Do you save old greeting cards and letters, or throw them all away? Why?
18. On a scale of 1 to 10, how well do you sing?
19. When you're alone at home, do you wear shoes, socks, slippers, or go barefoot?
20. What are the advantages and disadvantages of being your height?
21. When was the last picnic you went on? Describe it.

22. How many discount or savings coupons do you clip in an average month? How many expire before you use them?
23. Who's the biggest "pack rat" you know?
24. Whose autographs have you collected?
25. What's something you should throw away, but can't? Explain.
26. What food items did you eat so far today?
27. How often do you get a haircut? Describe your worst haircut.
28. How particular are you about the maintenance of your car?
29. Who's the most famous person you have ever met? What famous person would you most like to meet?
30. What is your most unusual nighttime or morning ritual?
31. How often do you read your horoscope? Do you believe there's any truth to it?
32. What kinds of movies do you most enjoy? Why?
33. When was the last time you stubbed your toe so hard it brought tears to your eyes?
34. How do you get rid of pesky phone calls from telemarketers?
35. What are you a "natural" at doing?
36. What's the story behind a time when you got locked out?
37. When's the last time you had to give a speech? How did it go?
38. How often do you get sick?
39. What's something valuable that you accidentally dropped and broke? Describe the situation.
40. What's the first thing that comes to mind when you hear the word "fun"?
41. At amusement parks, are you drawn more to the scariest roller coaster or the tamest merry-go-round? Why?
42. When's the last time you square-danced or line-danced? Rate your dancing ability on a scale of 1 to 10.
43. What are some of the wildest animals you've ever touched?
44. How many hours do you spend on your computer each day? How much time do you spend "surfing the Web"?
45. What makes you sick?
46. What has been your best work of art? Describe it.
47. What is something mischievous you have done?
48. When you leave a room, do you turn the lights off behind you or keep the lights on throughout your house most of the time? Explain your answer.
49. What's the worst tasting thing you've ever eaten?
50. When talking to someone while standing, are your arms

usually at your sides, in your pockets, crossed in front of you,or gesturing descriptively? Demonstrate your answer.

51. What magazines do you subscribe to, and how many of those do you actually read or look through? Do you throw any of them away unread?
52. Have you ever purchased anything from a telemarketer? If so, what was it? If not, why didn't you?
53. How frequently do you purchase lottery tickets or mail in sweepstakes registrations? Have you ever won anything from them?
54. What's the best New Year's resolution you've ever made?
55. When making an entrance into a social gathering, do you make your presence known so everyone notices you, slip in and look for someone you know, or sneak in as quietly as possible and find a safe spot to hide? Why?
56. How many hours a week do you watch TV? Is that too little, too much, or just enough?
57. What's your favourite kind of candy?
58. What's your strongest sense?
59. Are you most likely to finish your taxes as soon as you receive your W–2s or as close to April 15 as possible? How many times have you filed for an extension?
60. What can your friends predict you will grumble about most?
61. Do you prefer keeping the television channel remote in hand or giving it up? Why?
62. How many times a day do you look at your-self in the mirror?
63. When you travel, do you pack too much or too little? Explain.
64. What's the wackiest belief you held as a child?
65. What's your favourite beverage?
66. What are the best steps you've ever taken in an effort to improve your health?
67. When relaxing on the floor, do you sit cross-legged, fold your legs to one side, sit with your legs straight out in front of you, or recline?
68. Have you ever been an audience member for any television shows? Which ones? For which ones would you like to be an audience member?
69. What's one fashion trend you hope never comes back? Which ones have come back that you wish hadn't?
70. What magic tricks do you know? Perform one now.

71. What's the best (or funniest) commercial you've ever seen?
72. When was the last time you sat on a park bench for more than ten minutes? Describe the occasion.
73. What's the most embarrassing thing you've seen someone else do?
74. When something is funny, do you usually laugh raucously, hiss, snort, chuckle quietly to yourself, or smile and nudge the person next to you?
75. How important is it to you that people remember, spell, and pronounce your name correctly? Why?
76. What's your favourite item to cook? Why?
77. Do you usually send serious or humorous greeting cards? Why?
78. Would you ever be interested in observing a surgery or do you turn away when the nurse brings out the needle? Why?
79. Which movies have you watched over and over again?
80. What do you admire most about your best friend?
81. What was one vacation that lasted too long?
82. To feel rested, how many hours of sleep do you need each night?
83. What's one guilty pleasure you enjoy too much to give up?
84. Who performs more random acts of kindness than anyone else you know? Give the details.
85. What jingle comes to your mind? Hum or whistle it right now and see if others can correctly guess it!
86. How many credit cards do you have? How often do you use them?
87. How often do you leisurely eat a meal with friends?
88. Who's the jolliest person you know? Describe him or her.
89. What sound drives you crazy?
90. What sound lulls you to sleep?
91. Who's the smartest person you know?
92. What food do you eat for comfort?
93. How often do you read the newspaper? Which sections do you turn to first?
94. In one sentence, how would you describe your best friend?
95. How long, on average, does it take you to fall asleep once you turn out the lights?
96. What items do you currently have stored in the trunk of your car?
97. Which animals scare you most? Why?

98. What remedy for curing the common cold works best for you?
99. Where are you ticklish? How much does it bother you to be tickled?
100. Is the paper money in your possession right now organized sequentially according to denomination and with the bills right side up and facing the same way?Why or why not?

PERSONAL PROFILE

101. Are you a hugger or a non-hugger? Why?
102. What drives you crazy?
103. Are you serious-minded or a jokester? Why?
104. Are you more likely to avoid conflict or engage in it head-on? Why?
105. What was the most recent compliment you received and savored?
106. What's something about yourself that you hope will change, but that probably never will?
107. What's something about yourself that you hope will never change?
108. Are you a leader or a follower? How do you know?
109. Are you more of a rule breaker or a rule keeper? Why?
110. Would you describe yourself as an extrovert or an introvert? Give an example.
111. Would you describe yourself as more of a feeler or a thinker? Why?
112. Are you usually late, early, or on time? Why?
113. What goals have you recently set for yourself, and how are you doing on them so far?
114. To what degree are you patriotic? How do you express your patriotism?
115. Are you a creature of habit? Explain your answer.
116. In what situations are you most likely to procrastinate?
117. What books have made a big impact on you?
118. At what age do you hope to retire? Explain.
119. How much of a bargain hunter are you? Explain.
120. How much of a shopper are you? Where's your favourite place to shop?
121. Are you ever a high-maintenance person? Explain.

122. When was the last time you really pushed yourself to your physical limits? Explain.
123. What's one of your hobbies?
124. How much poetry have you written in your life?
125. How do you typically react in a sudden, extreme, pressure-filled crisis?
126. How do you go about illuminating "blind spots" in your life?
127. How mechanically inclined do you consider yourself? Give an example.
128. How many different conversations can you adequately carry on at the same time?
129. Are you a person who has a whole lot of acquaintances or just a few very close friends? Why?
130. How comfortable are you with uncertainty? Explain.
131. On a scale of 1 to 10, how computer savvy are you? Explain.
132. Are you superstitious? Give an example.
133. What one word best describes your mother?
134. What one word best describes your father?
135. Do you have a collection? If so, what do you collect and why?
136. When are you shy?
137. Do you tend to save everything or toss everything? Why?
138. What's something you regret losing, selling, or giving away? Explain why.
139. How absentminded do you get? Give an example.
140. Which is better: your short-term or your long-term memory?
141. What's your idea of cute?
142. Are you more inclined to "build your own empire" or "unleash the potential of others"? Explain.
143. What do you take for granted the most?
144. How often do you interrupt others while they are talking? Give a reason for your answer.
145. When you have nothing pressing, where does your mind drift?
146. What are your career goals?
147. How competitive are you? Explain.
148. Are you a penny-pincher or a big spender? Why?
149. Would you describe yourself as more laid back or more intense? Why?
150. Are you a risk taker? Why or why not?
151. Do you care more about pleasing people or speaking the truth? Explain your answer.

152. What inspires you to write?
153. What big challenge have you taken on recently?
154. When was the last time you wanted to scream? Explain.
155. Do you ever double or triple check things? If so, what?
156. What bores you?
157. What's someone's idiosyncrasy that really bothers you?
158. What's an idiosyncrasy or strange habit that you have?
159. On a scale of 1 to 10, how controlling a person are you? Explain.
160. What bad habit do you wish you could break?
161. On a scale of 1 to 10, how much of a perfectionist are you? Explain.
162. What's a strange occurrence you've observed but, until now, have never (or rarely) shared with anyone?
163. Where do you think you spend most of your money?
164. What do you think about more than anything else?
165. What books are you reading these days?
166. What allergies do you have?
167. How tolerant a person are you?
168. To what extent do others' beliefs influence you? Why?
169. To what degree do you consider yourself athletic? At which sports do you excel?
170. What causes you to get flustered?
171. At what time of the day do you feel your best?
172. What time do you usually wake up in the morning? Do you awaken naturally or need an alarm?
173. What fear would you like to overcome?
174. When do you most feel like a slave to time?
175. What do you consider your best quality?
176. Are you more task oriented or people oriented? Why?
177. How do you feel about your age?
178. Is it more important to you to look good or feel good? Explain.
179. What's your idea of a good time?
180. Are you a compulsive shopper or do you bring a list and carefully consider your purchases? Why?
181. Who is the first person you tell when some-thing good happens to you?
182. Whom do you run to when something bad happens in your life?
183. In what circumstances do your motor skills short-circuit your verbal skills, and vice versa?

184. In what situations are you most uncomfortable?
185. When are you the most at ease with yourself?
186. How good are you at multitasking? Give an example.
187. What do you do when you want to relax?
188. Are you an early bird or a night owl? Why?
189. What's something that amazes you?
190. Do you say "goodbye" quickly, slowly, or not at all? Why?
191. What spells adventure for you?
192. What tests the limits of your sense of balance?
193. How much of a "people watcher" are you? In what places do you find yourself "people watching"?
194. What do you like and dislike most about your current job?
195. Whom do you call when you need a hand?
196. What is your greatest physical challenge?
197. Under what circumstances is it impossible for you to sleep?
198. How do you best avoid conflict?
199. How accident-prone are you? Describe a recent incident.
200. What's the most important thing about you?

PREFERENCES

201. What's your favourite ice-cream brand and flavour?
202. What's your all-time favourite meal, and how often do you enjoy it?
203. What's your all-time favourite movie, and how many times have you seen it?
204. What's your dream job?
205. When you need to confront someone, would you rather communicate in person, on the phone, by e-mail, or by letter? Why?
206. Which do you prefer: the hustle and bustle of city life or the quiet and serenity of country life? Why?
207. Do you read or study best in silence or in a place with background noise? Why?
208. Do you prefer exercising your mind or your body? How frequently do you do either?
209. Do you prefer that people shoot straight with you or carefully temper their words? Why?
210. Are you more of a dog person or a cat person? Why?
211. What's your preference: plane, train, boat, automobile, horse, or camel?

212. How far in advance do you prefer to plan? Why?
213. What's your favourite board game? Do you usually win?
214. Who's your favourite talk show host?
215. Are you a traveller or a homebody? Explain.
216. Do you enjoy a good debate or prefer keeping the peace?
217. What was your favourite recess activity: Dodge ball, Kickball, Four Square, Hopscotch, Freeze Tag, or jump rope?
218. What's your favourite room in your home? Why?
219. Where's your perfect dream vacation spot?
220. Where's your favourite place to take out-of-town guests?
221. Do you prefer to thoroughly deliberate options or decisively draw conclusions? Why?
222. What is your favourite style of music, and how often do you listen to it?
223. What's your pick: hang glider, sky dive, bungee jump, hot air balloon, or kite?
224. Which of the five senses do you treasure most? Why?
225. When you find yourself in an argument, do you prefer to leave and resolve it later or stay and settle it right away? Why?
226. What's one thing you would rather pay someone to do than do yourself? Why?
227. What's one book you recommend and why?
228. What annoys you most about women?
229. What annoys you most about men?
230. What do you like most about women?
231. What do you like most about men?
232. What's your favourite genre of literature?
233. What's your preferred method of getting the news?
234. What's your favouritecolour? Why?
235. What's your favourite question to ask? What's your favourite question to answer?
236. What's your favourite expression?
237. What's your all-time favourite video game?
238. What real person, dead or alive, do you wish you could be more like? Why?
239. What's your all-time favourite band, and what would you give to meet them?
240. What's your least favourite thing to do? Why?
241. What's your favourite subject to discuss? Why?
242. When you fly, do you prefer to arrive at the airport extra early or get there just in the nick of time? Why?

243. Whom do you most admire? Why?
244. What bothers you most about perfectionists?
245. How do you prefer to give constructive criticism? Do you typically wait for someone to ask for it or not? Why?
246. What are your three favourite television shows? How frequently do you watch them?
247. Of all the tools and gadgets, you own, which one do you most enjoy using?
248. What is one of your favourite souvenirs brought back from your travels? Where do you keep it?
249. What's your choice: baseball, football, Frisbee, Hacky Sack, or boomerang?
250. What are the best and worst sounds in the world?
251. When you go to a movie, do you like to sit in the back, middle, or front? Why?
252. Where's your favourite spot from which to view the sunrise or sunset?
253. What's your most and least preferred forms of exercise? Explain.
254. Growing up, what was your favourite fairy tale or children's story? Why?
255. What's your choice: jigsaw, crossword, or numeric puzzles?
256. What is your favourite bumper sticker or t-shirt slogan?
257. What's your favourite aroma or fragrance?
258. What's your favourite spectator sport, and how often do you watch it?
259. What's one of your favourite summer activities to do with family or friends?
260. Do you prefer to plan your vacation or be spontaneous? Why?
261. What's your pleasure: horseshoes, shuffle-board, croquet, archery, or darts?
262. What are your favourite summer and winter sports?
263. What's your most treasured piece of jewellery? Why?
264. What's your reaction toward people who are outspoken about their beliefs? What conditions cause you to dislike or, conversely, enjoy talking with them?
265. What is something that bothers you if it is not done perfectly? Why is that so?
266. Who is your favourite musician, and how often have you seen him or her perform?
267. who's your favourite comedian?

268. What's your fancy: bird watching, butterfly collecting, flower hunting, shell gathering, or star gazing?
269. What's your favourite fast-food restaurant and how often do you go there?
270. What's the name of your favourite magazine? What do you like most about it?
271. What's the worst movie you've ever seen, and who did you see it with?
272. When driving, are you more likely to listen to the radio, to CDs and tapes, or nothing at all? Why?
273. What's your fancy: skateboard, roller blades, roller skates, ice skates, or snowboard?
274. What's your preferred way to meet new people? Explain.
275. Where's your favourite place to be? Why?
276. How do you prefer to learn or memorize new information?
277. What's your pleasure: tennis, badminton, volleyball, racquetball, or Ping-Pong?
278. What is your favourite day of the week? Why?
279. What's your favourite season of the year? Why?
280. When you are home alone, do you need the stereo, radio, or TV turned on? Or do you prefer the quiet? Explain.
281. What's your preference: wrestling, martial arts, boxing, or fencing?
282. Do you have a set place for everything at home or do you simply let things stay wherever they land? Give some examples.
283. Who's the best cook you know, and what's his or her specialty?
284. Who's the most creative or artistic person you know?
285. What's your preference: motorcycle, dirt bike, moped, mountain bike, racing bike, scooter, or unicycle?
286. What is your favourite poem or saying? Why is it your favourite?
287. What's your favourite quote? Why is it special to you?
288. Do you prefer window or aisle?
289. As you fall asleep, do you prefer to be flat on your back, curled on your side, or on your stomach? What position are you in when you wake up?
290. What type of museum do you most like to visit?
291. What strikes your fancy: zoo, circus, carnival, county fair, or parade?

292. What's your preference: cruise ship, powerboat, sailboat, rowboat, kayak, or inner tube?
293. What's your favourite holiday tradition? What meaning does it have for you?
294. Where's your favourite place to go when you want to be alone? Why?
295. Do you remember jokes very well? What's the best joke you've heard recently?
296. Who's your favourite person in the whole wide world? Why?
297. What's your all-time favourite town or city? Why?
298. Do you have a favourite painting or drawing? What makes it special to you?
299. What social issue fires you up?
300. What are the top three qualities that first draw you to someone new?

BLAST FROM THE PAST

301. What's one of your greatest achievements?
302. What's your favourite birthday memory?
303. Who was your best friend in high school, and where is he or she now?
304. What was your first job? How much did you get paid?
305. As a kid, what did you want to grow up to be?
306. What photos do you cherish from the past? Where do you keep them now?
307. Was there ever a time when it turned out you were right, despite many others who thought otherwise? Explain the situation.
308. What one word sums up your high school experience?
309. When was the last time you played hooky? Explain the situation.
310. As a child, what was your idea of fun?
311. When have you experienced poor customer service? How did you react?
312. What do you remember about your first day of school or your first teacher?
313. What's your most memorable (good or bad) airplane flight?
314. How many bones have you broken? Share the details.
315. What's something you've done that surprised even you?

316. How many times have you had stitches, and what were the circumstances? Explain.
317. What pets did you have growing up? What were their names?
318. Have you ever seen or called a psychic? What was your experience like?
319. Was school easy or difficult for you? How so?
320. What kind of kids did you hang out with in high school?
321. Who was your favourite teacher growing up, and what didyou like most about him or her?
322. What is the best bargain you ever found?
323. What's your most treasured heirloom?
324. Can you remember the address of one of your childhood homes? If so, what was it?
325. How have your priorities changed over time? Explain.
326. When did you get your first traffic ticket? Share the details.
327. What's the most dangerous situation you've encountered? How did you react?
328. How did someone plan a surprise for you? What was your reaction?
329. What was your favourite subject in school? Why?
330. Who has made the biggest impact on you? Explain.
331. Who has been your friend the longest? How and when did you meet him or her?
332. Did you or someone you know ever talk a police officer out of writing a ticket? Describe the situation.
333. Growing up, for which holidays did your family decorate the house?
334. Have you ever helped a total stranger? If so, how?
335. Growing up, what was your favourite comic strip?
336. What was an act of kindness you offered or received?
337. Have you dreamed of flying, falling, or running? Describe your most vivid memory of one of these dreams.
338. Have you ever had a premonition that came true? Explain.
339. Have you ever served on jury duty? If so, what was the case about? If not, would you like to be on a jury in the future?
340. Did a sibling or childhood peer ever tease or torment you? Share the details.
341. What childhood accident stands out in your mind?
342. When the "tooth fairy" came, what did you usually get?
343. What's your favourite picnic memory?

344. Who was your least favourite teacher? Why?
345. Have you ever been let off the hook for a punishment you deserved? How did that make you feel?
346. Did you ever cheat on a school exam? Describe the situation.
347. What was a childhood disillusionment you experienced?
348. As a child, did you take music lessons or take part in band or choir? Explain.
349. What "close call" did you have from the past? Describe it.
350. What's the best advice you've ever been given?
351. How much trouble did you get into during your school days? Explain.
352. As a child, did you ever peek into a wrapped gift before you actually received it? Did you ever get caught? Explain the details.
353. What dream has come true for you?
354. What's one of the biggest purchases you made, and how did you negotiate the transaction?
355. What is your earliest childhood memory?
356. What nightmare woke you up in a panic?
357. How has your birth order affected you?
358. Have you ever suggested an idea for change that was adopted? What was it?
359. What's the best prank you've ever pulled off?
360. What's the best prank someone pulled on you?
361. Growing up, for the most part, were you respectful or disrespectful to your parents? Explain.
362. What lasting lesson did you learn from your parents?
363. What was the last concert you attended? Who did you go with?
364. What one new thing did you learn in the last week?
365. How many foreign countries have you visited? Which one stands out in your memory?
366. How many American states have you visited in your lifetime? Which was your favourite and why?
367. What has frustrated you in the recent past? Explain.
368. In what sports, clubs, or activities were you most involved during high school?
369. Who was your first boyfriend or girlfriend? What was he or she like?
370. What is the first movie you saw in a theatre?

371. What was the name of your first album/CD?
372. What's something that you did growing up that your parents never found out about?
373. When were you in a situation where something struck you as funny, but it was inappropriate to laugh? What did you do to suppress your laughter?
374. What's a favourite memory with your grand-parents?
375. "Life is not measured by the number of breaths you take, but by the moments that take your breath away" (George Carlin). When have you had such a moment?
376. When were you in a hospital? Describe the situation.
377. Have you (or someone you know) ever been on national television? Describe the situation.
378. Have you ever participated in a long-distance walking, running, or biking event? Tell your story.
379. How many times did you move growing up? Describe your experience and how it impacted you.
380. What's the worst weather situation you've been in? Explain.
381. How would you describe your most magical childhood moment?
382. How would you summarize the highs and lows of this past week?
383. What was your best or worst job interview?
384. Have you ever had a challenging roommate situation? What was difficult about it?
385. What was your worst "nightmare" date?
386. What was your most romantic date?
387. What event in your life has brought about the greatest life-change?
388. What was one of your most frightening moments?
389. Was there ever a time when you or someone you know was a victim of fraud? Explain.
390. What was the best or worst job you ever had?
391. What outside influences have had the greatest impact on your family?
392. What's the best thing you ever built or created?
393. What's the story behind a time when a car you were in broke down?
394. What's the most adventurous or daring thing you have ever done?

395. What are your best or worst childhood memories of going to a zoo or circus?
396. What was a recent déjà vu experience?
397. Did you ever learn to swim? If so, how did you learn? Describe your experience.
398. How would you describe one of your happiest childhood memories?
399. What lesson did you have to learn the hard way?
400. When did you last have fresh flowers in your home? What was the occasion?

JUST IMAGINE

401. If you could be invisible for a day, what would you do?
402. If you could eliminate one weakness or limitation in your life, what would it be?
403. If you could change anything about your relationship with your parents, what would it be?
404. If you could switch job responsibilities with your boss, would you do it? Why or why not?
405. If you were able to retrieve only one item on the way out of your burning home, what would that be? Explain.
406. If you could go back in time, what year would you visit? Why?
407. If you could go anywhere for a one-day visit, where would you go? Why?
408. If you could spend one hour doing absolutely anything, what would you do?
409. If you had the opportunity to travel into space, would you go? Why or why not?
410. If you had an unlimited shopping spree at only one store, which one would you choose? Why?
411. If you could play any instrument, what would you choose? Why?
412. If you could talk with only one person for the rest of your life, who would it be and why?
413. If you could visit with any person in history, who would it be and why?
414. If you could do something very daring without fear, what would you do?
415. If you could take an early retirement, what would you do?

416. If you had the chance to go anywhere for dinner tomorrow, where would you go? Why?
417. If you were assured you would not fail, what endeavour would you attempt?
418. If you could be any celebrity, who would you want to become? Why?
419. If you won a million dollars in the lottery, how would you spend it?
420. If you had to perform a "Stupid Human Trick" for the David Letterman show, what would you do?
421. If you could learn to speak a foreign language, which one would you choose and why?
422. If you could change one thing about your appearance, what would it be?
423. If you could change one thing about your personality, how would you be different?
424. If you were stranded on a deserted island, what three "luxury items" would you most want to have with you?
425. If you could rule the world for one day, what would you do?
426. If you could change your occupation, what would you do?
427. If you could give one gift to your children, what would it be?
428. If you could live anywhere in the world, where would it be?
429. If you were able to listen to only one music CD ever again, what would it be and why?
430. If you were to write a book about your life, what would it be called?
431. If you were imprisoned and were allowed only one book to read, what would you choose and why?
432. If you could restore one broken relation-ship, which one would you choose? Why?
433. If you could bring one person back from the dead, who would you bring back? Why?
434. If you could live your life all over again, would you? Explain.
435. If you could possess it, what superhero's super power would you want to have and why?
436. If you had to change your first name, what name would you choose?
437. If you had the opportunity to start your own business, what would you start? Why?

438. If you could cure a disease or heal a sickness, which one would you choose? Why?
439. If you could bring peace to one country, which one would you select? Why?
440. If you could look into the future to find out one thing, what would you want to know?
441. If you could relive any year, what year would you choose? Why?
442. If you could have invented one thing, what would it have been?
443. If you could develop something that's not been invented yet, what would you invent?
444. If you were a WWE Smackdown champion wrestler, what would be your name and calling card?
445. If there were no animals in our world, what would we be missing?
446. If you were a master sculptor for a day, what would you sculpt?
447. If you were offered free cosmetic surgery by the best plastic surgeons in the world, would you take it? Explain.
448. If you could rob from the rich and give to the poor and get away with it, would you do it? Why?
449. If you could rid the world of one evil, which one would it be? Why?
450. If you were stranded on a deserted island, which three people would you most want to have join you?
451. If you could own any sports team, which one would it be?
452. If you had the ability to compete in the Olympics, what event would you want to be in?
453. If you had the talent to play a professional sport, which one would you select?
454. If you could establish one charitable organization, what would it be?
455. If you could turn into any animal at will, which one would you select? Why?
456. If you could read everyone's mind for one week only, would you tell anyone or keep it a secret? Explain.
457. If you could be a radio or television personal-ity, what kind of program would you choose?
458. If you oversaw ending world hunger, where would you start?

459. If you had the time to volunteer for any worthwhile organization, which one would you choose? Why?
460. If you had to design a float for a parade, what would you design?
461. If you could live forever on earth, would you choose to do so? Explain.
462. If you were to paint a picture of your child-hood, what colours would you use? Describe your picture.
463. If you were on a debate team, what subject would you relish debating?
464. If you could rid the world of one fear, what fear would it be? Why?
465. If you could write a best-selling book, what would you write about?
466. If you were a doctor, which field of medicine would you specialize in? Why?
467. If you could change one thing about the culture you live in, what would it be? Why?
468. If you were required to distribute a million dollars any way you wanted, how would you do it?
469. If you were to star in a movie, what would be your ideal role?
470. If you could rewrite history, what one thing would you change?
471. If you were forced to give up one of your five senses, which one would you choose? Why?
472. If you had to choose right now, who would you select to be in your wedding party?
473. If you were a gifted painter, what picture would you want to paint first?
474. If you could give some advice to all parents, what would you say?
475. If you had to do your life over, what one thing would you do differently? Explain.
476. If you could be any cartoon character, which one would you be?
477. If you could make any improvement on how cars operate, what would it be?
478. If you could teach any class on any subject, what would you teach and to whom would you teach it?
479. If you could wave a magic wand and stop any one thing, what would you stop? Why?

480. If you could ask any question of the people you're with right now and get an honest answer, what question would you ask?
481. If you could trade places with anyone for one week, who would you want to trade with and why?
482. If you could make one character from any work of fiction come to life, what character would you select?
483. If you were a great explorer, what would you explore?
484. If you could be a contestant on any game show, which one would it be?
485. If you found an abandoned car with $50,000 in the back seat, what would you do?
486. If you could own a restaurant, what kind would it be?
487. If you could run Hollywood, what would you do?
488. If you could transport yourself at will between any two destinations, which two would you choose? Why?
489. If you could redecorate your home at no cost, what would you wish to do?
490. If you could be any age for the rest of your life, what age would you choose? Why?
491. If you could capture any event in history on videotape, which one event would it be?
492. If you were to get a tattoo, what would it be? And where would you put it?
493. If you could grant any three wishes to one person, to whom would you grant them? Why?
494. If you were going to a costume party next week, what costume would you wear?
495. If you could take back something you've said, what would it be?
496. If you were to fast-forward your life five years, where would you be and what would you be doing? What changes would people see in you?
497. If you could say anything to the people you're with right now, what would you say?
498. If you were given $100,000 to celebrate some-one or something, who or what would you celebrate?
499. If you could give one piece of advice to pass on to the next generation, what would it be?
500. If you could hang a motto in every home, what would it say?

VIEW POINTS

501. What does "success" mean to you?
502. Do you think there will ever be world peace? Why or why not?
503. What's the secret to a long life?
504. Which is the greater tragedy: an innocent person imprisoned, or a guilty person set free? Explain.
505. How important is it to set personal goals?
506. Are people trustworthy? Explain your answer.
507. What is beauty?
508. Why do you think people live in denial?
509. What new law is needed to make the world a better place to live?
510. How would you describe the perfect day?
511. In your opinion, what is the moral condition of this world?
512. Why do you think divorce is so prevalent?
513. What is the ideal age to get married? Why?
514. To what extent is knowledge power, to what extent is truth power, and what's the difference?
515. Do you believe that the human soul is eternal?
516. What is the greatest invention the world has ever seen?
517. What do you think is needed to make the world a better place?
518. What advice can you give about how to conquer fear?
519. What advice can you give about how to relieve stress?
520. Why are some people cruel and unkind?
521. What is the difference between knowing a lot of facts about a person and knowing someone personally?
522. What do you think is the secret to a happy marriage?
523. Why do innocent people suffer?
524. Why do bad things happen to good people?
525. Do you believe that, for the most part, people are basically good, basically bad, or a mixture? Why?
526. Is seeking truth a way of life or a season of life? Explain.
527. Do you believe ignorance is bliss? Why or why not?
528. Why do you think it's so hard for people to say they're sorry?
529. When does the end justify the means?
530. What do you think is the greatest problem of humans?
531. Why are bad habits so hard to break?
532. Whom do you consider the greatest president of all time? Why?

533. What is truth?
534. What's more important, a healthy mind or a healthy body? Why?
535. What makes a true friendship?
536. Does life imitate art or does art imitate life? Explain.
537. What is "unconditional forgiveness"?
538. To what extent is it possible to show respect or tolerance and still disagree?
539. What does it mean when two people are said to have "chemistry"?
540. Do you think science will offer the "final answer" to all the world's problems? Why or why not?
541. To what extent is cloning a moral issue? Explain.
542. When is it better to be safe than sorry?
543. What does it mean to be powerful?
544. What is the benefit of meditation?
545. Why is it sometimes hard to forgive others?
546. What's most intriguing about the Cinderella story?
547. How well do you receive criticism from others? Why do most people fear honest feedback and evaluation?
548. What does this quote mean? "He is no fool who gives what he cannot keep, to gain what he cannot lose." (Jim Elliot)
549. What's the best approach for resolving conflict?
550. Which is more important: what you say or how you say it? Explain your answer.
551. Do you think a sixth sense exists? Explain.
552. Do you think the end, or the means is most important? Explain.
553. When is it appropriate to resort to making a threat? When is a threat not a threat?
554. What role does trust play in our everyday relationships?
555. What's the best way to earn another person's respect?
556. When is it necessary to take the law into your own hands?
557. What is the basis of your standard of right and wrong?
558. What's the best way to win back an estranged friend?
559. What's the best way to resist peer pressure?
560. Which is greater, love of one's parents, one's children, one's spouse, or one's friends? Explain your answer.
561. What do you think is the most significant event in the history of the human race? Explain.

562. How would you define "freedom"?
563. What are the best ways to inspire or motivate people?
564. What's the best way to delegate things to others?
565. In raising children, do you think it's best to discipline by giving timeouts, discussions, spankings, or a combination? Why?
566. What's the best way to negotiate a raise in salary?
567. Where do you draw the line between helping people and showing them how to help them-selves? How do you strike that balance?
568. What's a sure way to detect when someone is lying?
569. How do you measure contentment?
570. Why do some people resist living lives of moral integrity?
571. What's the best way to handle another person's hostility and ease tensions?
572. How important is physical appearance when it comes to achieving success or getting one's way in life?
573. Is cloning a sign of progress? Why or why not?
574. What's the age of accountability?
575. What is the secret to being content in all circumstances?
576. Who's the greatest leader of all time? Why?
577. Does work really banish three great evils— boredom, vice, and poverty? Explain.
578. What do you recommend overcoming self-pity?
579. If you did something wrong, would it make any difference that you did so unintentionally? Would you still be morally responsible? Explain.
580. How do you define "true love"?
581. What's the best approach to use in negotiating a fair purchase price for a car?
582. How do you suggest overcoming negative self-talk?
583. Why is it taboo to discuss personal financial matters?
584. What's the best remedy for anxiety caused by speaking in front of a large group of people?
585. When is failure a success?
586. Is there such a thing as a "just war"? Explain.
587. What's your position on capital punishment?
588. What is the meaning of life?
589. Why is life so hard? Why is life so complicated?
590. What's unforgivable?

591. If accumulation of money doesn't bring lasting happiness, what does?
592. Why are people who win the lottery often unhappier than they were before their win?
593. What happens after death?
594. What is it about human nature that tends to stubbornly refuse the aid of someone else?
595. What is the difference between an intellectual assent to a set of beliefs and an actual acceptance of those beliefs?
596. What purpose do the emotions of regret, shame, or guilt serve?
597. Do you think religious holidays have become too commercialized by society? Why or why not?
598. Do you think the general population is better off or worse off than it was fifty years ago? Why?
599. What's the difference between intelligence and wisdom?
600. What's one thing you know for sure?

HARD-HITTING

601. What's one regret you live with?
602. What do you live in denial about?
603. What phobias have you struggled with?
604. How difficult is it for you to forgive someone who refuses to apologize?
605. What's the most serious illness or injury you ever faced?
606. How are you different now than you were before September 11, 2001?
607. How would you prefer to die—quickly without warning or slowly over time?
608. What insults your intelligence?
609. What's one conviction you hold that you would be willing to die for?
610. When is it okay to lie?
611. What's your most embarrassing moment?
612. When have you had to agree to disagree? Explain.
613. What bad habit have you broken?
614. In an emergency, which friends would you feel the freedom to call in the middle of the night?
615. Where are you going?
616. What impossible task are you facing right now?
617. What fear are you trying to overcome?

618. Would most people describe you as humble or proud? Why?
619. Have you ever violated a confidence? Describe what happened.
620. Have you ever been falsely accused? Describe the situation and how you felt about it.
621. What character trait are you currently trying to improve or change?
622. Have you ever gotten caught doing some-thing you shouldn't have done? Describe the occasion.
623. Was there ever a time when you were very sure of something, but were later proved wrong? Explain what happened and how you reacted.
624. If you just found out you had only two weeks to live, what top two or three things would you do? Why?
625. What do you suspect people say about you behind your back?
626. How have you been humbled? Describe the details.
627. When was the last time you said, "It's my fault—I'm sorry"? Explain the situation.
628. What scares you the most about the future?
629. What hot topic usually turns into an argument with you?
630. In what situation do you often find yourself "walking on eggshells"?
631. What traumatic event has changed your life forever?
632. Who's the "black sheep" of your family? Explain the situation.
633. What one person in your life do you find the most challenging? Explain.
634. What temptation have you successfully resisted? Describe the situation.
635. What's something about you that no one knows?
636. How do you comfort those who have suffered a tragedy or loss?
637. How difficult is it for you to speak the truth, even when it may be hurtful or unpopular?
638. What was the hardest era of your life?
639. Have you found your place in this world? If so, where is it?
640. If you died today, who would give your eulogy, and what would be said?
641. What one thing do you fear more than any-thing else?
642. How afraid of dying are you? Explain.

643. What's something for which you would seek revenge?
644. What was your last argument about?
645. How often do you tell little white lies? Give an example.
646. What is your greatest weakness?
647. How do you explain death?
648. What epitaph would you want engraved on your tombstone?
649. What kinds of things do you catch yourself exaggerating about?
650. What lie did you tell today?
651. Have you ever felt like you were taking three steps forward but two steps back? Explain.
652. What's the closest you've come to having an epiphany?
653. What would make you totally content right now?
654. What is something that you failed at?
655. What mystery have you solved?
656. When you think of really living and not merely existing, what comes to mind?
657. What's something you consider too daring to try?
658. How at peace are you with yourself? Explain.
659. Would you want to know the date and cause of your death? How would that information change things for you?
660. What is the hardest thing you've ever done?
661. What do you think is your purpose in life?
662. What's the most ridiculous thing you've ever stolen? Explain the situation.
663. What paradox (or contradiction) in life have you had to learn to accept or embrace?
664. To what extent are you an argumentative person? Explain.
665. Why are we here?
666. To what extent do you trust people? Explain.
667. Would you ever give up your life for a friend or family member? Why or why not?
668. If you knew your death could save a stranger's life, would you give up your life? Why or why not?
669. What do you hope to discover beyond the grave?
670. What lesson has failure taught you?
671. Is your "glass" usually half full or half empty? Why?
672. What's the most significant loss you've experienced?
673. What's the closest you've ever come to thinking you didn't deserve to live? Explain.

674. What's an example of your passive-aggressive side?
675. How do you know this world is not a dream? Can you prove it?
676. Have you forgiven yourself for past personal failures? Why or why not?
677. In what area of your life are you immature?
678. How do you deal with very needy people?
679. How do you most want to be remembered?
680. Did you ever witness someone die? Describe your thoughts and feelings at that time.
681. What important competition have you lost?
682. What do you hope will be your biggest life-time contribution to society?
683. What do you do to get "centered"?
684. Have you ever broken or spilled something in someone else's home? Did you try to cover it up or fix it so it would go unnoticed? Explain.
685. How healthy or unhealthy are you with setting boundaries? Explain.
686. "I do what I don't want to do and I don't do what I want to do." To what extent do you relate to that statement? Explain.
687. Do you ever fear "living" as much as "dying"? Explain.
688. Was there ever a time when your blood "ran cold?" Explain.
689. How have you dealt with loss in your life?
690. Is there such a thing as "destiny"? Why or why not?
691. How would you graciously turn down an invitation to go out on a date? How would you graciously break up with someone you were dating?
692. What positives, if any, have resulted from the suffering you've experienced in your life?
693. How do you deal with doubt?
694. What holds you back?
695. What negative behavioral pattern has been passed down from generation to generation within your family?
696. What brings out your pessimistic side?
697. What's missing in your life? What one thing would make your life complete?
698. How convinced are you that the sun will rise tomorrow? What makes you so sure?
699. Who are you when no one's looking?
700. How hard is life? How does your life compare?

FROM THE HEART

701. When was the last time you cried? Why?
702. How would you describe a time when you felt alone in a crowd?
703. What makes you stand to your feet and cheer?
704. On a scale from 1 to 10, how happy do you usually feel? Explain.
705. What's your most prized or sentimental possession? Explain.
706. What or who inspires you to be all that you can be?
707. When have you been overwhelmed with compassion or overcome with pity? How were you transformed by the experience?
708. What in this world breaks your heart?
709. If you had to locate the feeling of "longing" or "yearning" in your body, where would you say it was?
710. Describe a time when you lost something very valuable. How did you feel when you finally found it or when you realized it would never be found?
711. How do you handle anger?
712. What stresses you out?
713. What is something that always brings a smile to your face?
714. What mood are you usually in? Explain why.
715. What silly thing have you done in the name of love?
716. When was the last time you helped someone in need? Describe it.
717. What's one accomplishment that gives you great satisfaction?
718. What was your proudest moment?
719. In relationships, are you more often the "heartbreaker" or the "heart broken"? Why?
720. How many times have you really been in love?
721. How many times have you had a broken heart?
722. Whom have you lost touch with but still wonder about?
723. How have you honoured your parents?
724. What's the most cowardly thing you've ever done?
725. Who has loved you more than anyone else in your life?
726. What was the happiest era of your life?
727. What's the most courageous thing you've ever done?
728. When have you recently felt overwhelmed? Describe the situation.
729. What one thing do you wish for more than anything else?
730. What do you dream about most often? How do you interpret your dreams?

731. What's the best greeting card you ever received?
732. How have you significantly honoured another person?
733. What has recently made you depressed?
734. Have you ever felt excluded? Explain the situation and how it made you feel.
735. What was the best surprise you've ever pulled off?
736. What was the best news you've ever received?
737. When did you ever immediately "click" with someone you just met? What was the long-term result? To what do you attribute that kind of connection?
738. Was there ever a time when you were in need and someone met that need? Describe.
739. Is it better to have loved and lost or never to have loved at all? Explain.
740. What prevents you from revealing your emotions to others? Give an example.
741. What brings a tear to your eye?
742. When do you find yourself singing?
743. What colour describes your mood right now?
744. Is there a family tradition that has a special meaning for you? Describe it.
745. Of the following ways, how do you most like to express your love to another person: touch, words, gifts, time spent together, or acts of kindness?
746. Of the following ways, how do you most like to receive expressions of love: touch, words, gifts, time spent together, or acts of kindness?
747. When do you feel the loneliest?
748. What makes you feel like pulling the covers back over your head and staying hidden in bed all day long?
749. What brings out your critical side?
750. What fuels you?
751. What poem or song really moves you? Share a line from it.
752. What's one thing that makes you angry? Explain.
753. From what do you secretly long to be "rescued"?
754. What do you need to feel secure?
755. What was the greatest day of your life?
756. When you feel sad, what do you do to find comfort?
757. What objects from your childhood have you saved? Explain why.
758. Are you ever satisfied? Why or why not?

759. Do you use the word "love" freely and often or selectively and seldom? Explain why.
760. What's weighing heavy on your heart these days?
761. What do you do when a homeless person asks you for money? How do you feel afterward?
762. When you are happy, how do you like to celebrate?
763. How self-centred are you?
764. When have you had a cathartic experience and what was the impetus?
765. Is it better to love or be loved? Why?
766. Do you believe in "love at first sight"? Why or why not?
767. Do you believe in "soul mates"? Why or why not?
768. How is your love for your friends different from your love for your family?
769. What recent disappointment have you had?
770. When is the right time to demonstrate "tough love"?
771. Is there someone in your life who has never (or rarely) let you down? How long have you known this person?
772. When do you feel insecure?
773. To what extent do you trust your own judgment or gut instincts? Why?
774. What worries you?
775. How do you heal a broken heart?
776. Who have you loved more than anyone else in your life? Explain.
777. What do you want?
778. When was the last time your heart skipped a beat? Describe the situation.
779. When have you felt like you could "never repay" someone? Explain.
780. What does silence feel like to you?
781. What makes you feel jealous?
782. When was the last time your heart was in your throat? Describe the situation.
783. Was there ever a time when someone rescued you? Describe the closest thing that comes to mind.
784. Was there ever a time when you gave your heart completely over to something or someone? Describe the closest thing that comes to mind.
785. How often do you second-guess yourself? Why?
786. What situations cause you to hold back and protect your heart?

787. Have you ever felt like there was no escape; that your heart was trapped? Describe.
788. When have you felt betrayed?
789. What's your most cherished romantic moment?
790. What fills your heart up to the bursting level?
791. When do you feel out of control?
792. Has your heart ever lied to you, or do you think it always "tells" the truth? Explain.
793. When was a time when you felt honoured? Describe the situation.
794. How often or easily do movies make you cry?
795. What's one question you are asking yourself these days?
796. Growing up, what virtue did you see in your parents that you hope to emulate?
797. How sensitive a person are you? Explain.
798. What part of your heart has never been seen by anyone? Why?
799. Have you ever had someone do something for you or give something to you that you did not earn or deserve? Describe the situation and how it made you feel.
800. What makes your heart beat fast?

SPIRITUALLY SPEAKING

801. Why do you think there are so many different religions in the world?
802. Do you think that all the major religions are fundamentally the same or different? Explain your answer.
803. Do you think religion is an emotional crutch for some people? Why or why not?
804. What do you think heaven is like?
805. What do you think most people think about the Bible?
806. What do you think are the most common misconceptions people have about God?
807. Do you believe the Bible is actually God's chosen tool for communication to mankind? Why or why not?
808. Do you believe in reincarnation? Why or why not?
809. What do you like most about church, synagogue, or mosque?
810. Why does God seem so distant?
811. Do you think most people are spiritually attuned or spiritually ignorant?
812. What is your attitude toward people who believe differently than you?

813. Do you think God exists? Why or why not?
814. If God did not exist, what practical difference would that make in our world?
815. Is God dead? Explain.
816. Why do you think some people are skeptical about the existence of God? Why are others so certain he does exist?
817. Is belief in God intellectual suicide? Why or why not?
818. Do you think it's possible for anyone to know for sure if there is a God? Explain.
819. Why do you think that some form of religious belief is present in virtually every culture?
820. What do you like least about religion?
821. Do you think religion is necessary? Why or why not?
822. What are some characteristics you have heard taught about God that you do not believe?
823. Do you think religion should be a private matter? Why or why not?
824. Do you believe in miracles? Why or why not?
825. Do you believe God is actively involved in our world or detached and distant from our world? Explain.
826. How reliable do you think the Bible is as a historical document? Explain.
827. How would you explain eternity?
828. How many different religions have you studied in your lifetime, and which one makes the most sense to you right now? Explain.
829. Do you believe in an afterlife? Why or why not?
830. How do you think the afterlife will be different from this life?
831. How do you "remember your spirit"?
832. What does "being spiritual" mean to you?
833. Do you think most, if not all, wars would cease if no religious differences existed? Why or why not?
834. Are natural disasters God's doing? Explain.
835. How often do most people you know think about spiritual issues? Explain your answer.
836. If God decided to visit the planet right now, what do you think he would say or do?
837. Why do you think there are so many disagree-ments over spiritual and religious matters?
838. How do you picture the face of God?
839. Is your image of God more like that of a "grandfather," a "policeman," or a "mechanic"? Explain.

840. What's the central difference between psychology and religion, or do they address the same need in mankind? Explain.
841. What about God do you hope is true? Why?
842. What's the difference between being moral and being spiritual?
843. Do you think that scientific discoveries will eventually eliminate mankind's "need" for God? Why or why not?
844. What's the greatest spiritual advice you have ever received?
845. Given the pros and cons associated with deeply held religious beliefs, do you think that "religion" overall is a positive or a negative thing?
846. Do you believe that a spiritual realm exists outside of what can be perceived by the five senses? Why or why not?
847. How would you define "faith"?
848. Should faith in God be "blind" or should it require evidence? Explain.
849. What does it mean to take a "leap of faith"? Have you ever taken one?
850. Do you believe it is possible to encounter God in a personal way? Why or why not?
851. What, if anything, is the Bible good for?
852. What determines how much trust you will place in a spiritual authority?
853. Do you think a person, in order to be a certain religion, must be converted into that religion, born into it, or both?
854. How much influence has your family heritage had on your ultimate religious beliefs? Explain.
855. What is it that bothers you the most about religious fanatics?
856. What are the positives and negatives of joining a small group to discuss spiritual issues?
857. What did you like and dislike about any church services you've experienced?
858. Why did God start it all?
859. If you could design your own church service, what would it look like?
860. How many different paths do you think there are to God? Explain.
861. What is the difference between "faith" and "religion"?
862. Why does merely talking about Christianity often muster up negative images and angry reactions?
863. Generally speaking, does Christianity, with its apparent emphasis on sin, hell, and judgment, dwell too much on the negative? Explain your answer.

864. What are the various ways people attempt to earn God's forgiveness or favour?
865. What is one thing you no longer believe about God that you believed when you were younger? What changed your mind?
866. What's one benefit the world has gained because of Jesus Christ's life and teaching ministry?
867. What's one benefit the world has gained because of Muhammad's life and teaching ministry?
868. What's one benefit the world has gained because of Buddha's life and teaching ministry?
869. What's your basis for deciding which, if any, religion is right for you?
870. Do you believe there is anything to the "power of prayer"? Explain.
871. From where does evil come?
872. Why is there so much evil in the world?
873. What do you think are some methods God uses to communicate to people?
874. Do you believe it's possible for people to communicate with the dead?
875. Do you believe an evil spiritual being, such as the Devil, exists? Why or why not?
876. What is it about the Bible that most confuses you?
877. What is your position concerning the concept of hell?
878. If God can do anything, can he make a rock so heavy he cannot lift it? Explain.
879. How good do you have to be to get into heaven?
880. Can a person know for sure that he or she is going to heaven? Why or why not?
881. Do you think all religions lead to God? Why or why not?
882. What's the difference between tolerance of all religions and validation of all religions?
883. Do you think that for one religion to be totally true, all other religions must be false? Explain.
884. Do you think that ultimately, no matter what we believe about God, we will all end up at the same place in order we are sincere? Explain your answer.
885. If the world contained no religion, how might things be different?
886. How do you react to a religious person who attempts to proselytize you?

887. How do you define a cult?
888. Can anyone know for sure that his or her religion is right? Explain.
889. What is your definition of a miracle?
890. If a bona fide miracle were to occur in your life, do you think that would convince you that intelligent Supreme Being exists? Why or why not?
891. Why do you think most people find it difficult, if not impossible, to believe in miracles?
892. Do you think angels and demons exist? Why or why not?
893. What do you think angels are like, and what is their function here on earth?
894. Do you believe you have a guardian angel?
895. What is the greatest commandment?
896. What is the greatest sin?
897. Why do some people become uncomfortable discussing spiritual matters?
898. What factors have most influenced your current beliefs about God?
899. What does God want from us?
900. If you could ask God to do any three things for you, and you knew he would do them, what would you ask him to do?

EXTREME SPIRITUAL MATTERS

901. When and how often do you pray? What motivates you to pray.
902. On a scale from 1 to 10, how close to God do you feel? Explain.
903. Rate the level of intensity you have about wanting to know God? Explain your answer.
904. If a dimmer switch could represent your understanding of Christianity, how bright would your light be?
905. Has there ever been a time you were convinced you received direction from God? Describe it.
906. How do you discern God's direction for your life?
907. How has your belief or disbelief in God affected your life?
908. What fears do you have about God?
909. What makes it difficult for you to trust God?
910. If you were to explain to a friend what it means to know God personally, what would you say?
911. With everything in this universe that could consume God's time and energy, how much do you think God really cares about what happens in your life?

912. What is your greatest fear about what you'd be like if God were leading your life?
913. Why doesn't God do something about evil and suffering?
914. When have you experienced a situation in which you believe God intervened? Describe it.
915. What is your reaction to the Bible's claim that Jesus is the only way to God?
916. What has been your biggest obstacle to spiritual growth?
917. Where are you in your spiritual journey?
918. Using the compartments of a car, how would you describe where God fits into your life (trunk, driver's seat, back seat, glove compartment, passenger seat, etc.)? Explain your answer.
919. What prevents you from taking steps on your spiritual journey now?
920. Who will be in heaven? Why?
921. If God were to step in and wipe out every trace of evil, what would that do to the human population? Where would that leave you?
922. When have you seen "hell" here on earth?
923. Why do you suppose God doesn't just eliminate Satan now?
924. Where was God when terrorists attacked the World Trade Centre and the Pentagon?
925. If you were to die today, would you go to heaven? On what do you base your answer?
926. If you could prove beyond a reasonable doubt that God exists, do you think you would seek out a relationship with him?
927. If you believed in the God of the Bible, do you think it would impact the way you lived? Why or why not?
928. Have you ever had something you would call a "spiritual experience"? Describe the situation.
929. What religious issues are you struggling with these days?
930. What kinds of things do you pray about most frequently?
931. What personal religious experiences have had the most profound impact on you?
932. How certain are you that your current belief about God is correct? What would change that?
933. What do you think is the difference between a religious person who makes it into heaven and one who does not?
934. Do you think it is possible for a man to gain the whole world and yet lose his soul? Explain.
935. What does it mean to be made in the "image of God"?

936. What would you suggest would be the best way for God to show his love?
937. What's your favourite Bible verse and why?
938. What's the most reassuring Bible promise you know? Explain your answer.
939. Was there ever a time when you sincerely wanted to know God's will regarding a decision you needed to make? What was the outcome? Describe the situation.
940. What season are you currently in regarding your spiritual life?
941. What surprises you most about Jesus Christ?
942. According to your understanding, how would you summarize the central message of Christianity?
943. What's something most of your friends don't know about your spiritual side?
944. What do you think God would say to you right now?
945. What do you think God will say to you when you die?
946. Why do you think Jesus was born? Why were you born?
947. What's one thing about the existence (or nonexistence) of God that scares you?
948. The Bible says, "God is love." What does that mean to you?
949. Who is Jesus Christ to you?
950. What's the first question you will have for God when you die?
951. Who's the closest thing to a spiritual mentor to you?
952. How has God demonstrated his love to you?
953. What has produced the greatest spiritual growth in your life?
954. Have you ever prayed a prayer of desperation? Describe the situation.
955. How have you been disillusioned by religion?
956. How comfortable are you discussing spiritual things with others?
957. How is it possible that the death of one (Jesus Christ) overcomes (forgives) the sins of many (the whole human race)?
958. Do you think it is possible to have a false sense of security about your eternal destiny? Explain.
959. What do you think it means to be "born again"? What's your knee-jerk reaction to this term?
960. Is there something spiritual missing in your life? Explain.
961. Do you agree with this statement: "Going to church doesn't make you a Christian any more than going to a garage makes you an automobile" (Billy Sunday)? Why or why not?

962. How would you define sin?
963. What are the repercussions of sin, if any?
964. Do you think it is possible to be indifferent or neutral toward God without offending him?
965. What is your biggest personal spiritual dilemma or challenge?
966. What do you think was the purpose of Jesus Christ's death?
967. What reasons do you think Christianity gives for its assertion that Jesus is the only way to God?
968. In what ways is the Christian life difficult or impossible to live?
969. How has God changed you?
970. What do you think God's attitude is toward you?
971. Do you think becoming a Christian is an ongoing process, something that happens at a specific point in time, or a combination of the two? Give reasons for your answer.
972. Why should God let you into heaven?
973. Do you think God has ever used pain and suffering to get your attention? If so, what was he trying to get across to you?
974. How confident are you about what will happen to you in the afterlife? Explain.
975. Do you have any fears about being wrong about your spiritual beliefs? Explain.
976. If you were face-to-face with Jesus, what would he say to you? Give a reason for your answer.
977. Can hell, God's justice, and God's love all be real at the same time? Explain your answer.
978. How comfortable would you feel about praying out loud with someone? Why?
979. How do you distinguish God's voice from your own thoughts?
980. What miracle do you wish God would perform right now?
981. What's one doubt you have regarding the existence of a Supreme Being?
982. What would Jesus do if he were in your shoes?
983. When have you experienced the closest thing to a miracle? Describe it.
984. If you were to identify someone as a Christian, what definitive factors would you look for to support that claim?
985. Have you ever meditated for spiritual purposes? If so, describe your experience.
986. Have you ever been baptized? What does the sacrament of baptism mean to you?

987. How do you "feed your spirit"?
988. What's the closest you've come to having an encounter with God? Describe it.
989. To what extent is your view of God influenced by your view of your father?
990. For what are you most thankful to God?
991. In your opinion, is the Christian message mostly "good news" or mostly "bad news"? Explain your response.
992. When was a prayer of yours answered? Tell about it.
993. How frequently, if ever, do you read the Bible? What motivates you to read the Bible?
994. What's one thing about God you don't understand?
995. Do you make comparisons with others on a spiritual level? Why or why not?
996. How would you describe your own moral condition?
997. Do you believe sin causes a gap between God and you? Why or why not?
998. Do you ever become angry with God when things go wrong? Why or why not?
999. Do you find it easy to ignore or avoid facing up to deep spiritual matters? Why or why not?
1000. In what ways do your religious beliefs impact the way you live your life?
1001. If you could ask God one question you knew he would answer right away, what would it be?

4

Current Topics with Sample Answers

1. ARE DIGITAL PAYMENTS SECURE ENOUGH FOR THE INDIAN ECONOMY TO GO CASHLESS?

Points to remember before you participate in this discussion:

Assume, you one of the member of a real group discussion.

Take the initiative to participate and contribute your thoughts.

Express your positive attitude towards providing the solution.

Prerna said:

Use of digital payments are partially enough as India focuses on inclusive growth, but this facility of government can be utilised only by middle or elite section of society. Now also there are many places that are lacking this internet facility. 37% of people are still below poverty line. They even don't have proper food to eat then what they will think of buying android mobiles or having net connection. Benefits are there of using digital payments like Inc. In transparency, reduction in black money and corruption, financial inclusion but this all can only be possible if technological system is improved and everyone can afford smart phones.

Thank you.

Shrasti Aggarwal said:

Hello.

Yes, digital payments are secure enough for the country to go cashless. Since digital payments are fast and safe. It also helps the economy to overcome the corruption problem. There is a need for call of special training program to make aware how digital payments system works, benefits regarding digital payments etc.

Bhuvana said:

During demonetization usage of digital payments had increased a lot. Our honourable prime minister also suggested going cashless. Yes, I agree with digital payments because it helps to reduce corruption or black money. This notion is reaching to metropolitan areas then what about the villages.

Nitin said:

Hi friends,

In India, many people are corrupted in our country. So, our government take a good step to make our country cashless. And using digital system provided by the government like ATM card etc. But many problems can face by the people of our country because they don't know about the online paying. But they know that our government step is good to make our country cashless.

Ritika Rana said:

Yeah, I think so because it helps especially middle-class people to save their money through several taxes that are applied by the salesman to a customer. And even it saves time and efforts.

Vineetha said:

Hi friends,

After the action initiated by the honourable Prime Minister Narendra Modi, many people supported this act because it will stop the flow of black money, fake currency, etc. But some poor people have faced many problems because they don't even have ATM's to use. But later, all the people believes that it was great acts provided by the government. It made that India as a digital country.

Arvind said:

In my point of view digital payments are secure enough for the Indian economy to go cashless.After demonetization digital payments and transaction has increased, it shows that economy of India moving forward to go cashless. Now these days all digital payments are secured by many security systems that no one can miss use the others credentials while paying digitally. Indian government is also promoting the digital payment.

But Indian economy can't become cashless it will take many years to go cashless because in India rural areas people are not so much knowledge about digital payment, Indian government should take steps towards this type of problem.

Chandan said:

Hi

According to my point of view, Digital payment is a good way to the growing of economics India.

Because there is some black money are reduced and reduce corruption.

There is more beneficial for us that it saves time, and secure I know today in India someone doesn't know how to operate digital and a problem if any hacker hacks your account, and also a problem in digital payment if server is not working proper ways. So, my conclusion is about the digital topic is very well and some bad because everything is not perfect.

Ashish Signage said

Hi friends,

My name is Ashish.

According to me digital payments have been more secured continuously.

I hope, it will be totally secured in further 5 to 6 years and we will do our online or digital transaction more securely.

I think nowadays our online transaction is more secure than previous 10 years.

For ex:

On each and every transaction they (bank, online portals etc) will provide us one OTP (one-time password) on our registered mobile number. And only we can access this OTP at the time of transaction. So, we will be confident about our transaction that our money goes to authorized person. It wasn't happened 10 years back. So, we have continuously secured day by day. It will also reduce our cost of paper currency and we will do our transaction in a minute. And in the country like India, to go cashless is very essential because India is top at corruption level among other 207 country.

Rishi Jain said:

For the Indian economy to go fully cashless, the problem of security is secondary compared to the extent of digital illiteracy among the lower strata of Indian society, and the difficult access to banking services.

The government of India is taking phenomenal initiatives to promote Digital India, which had 3 primary objectives:

1) Improve the digital infrastructure in India and provide high-speed internet to rural areas.
2) Improve the digital literacy among Indians.
3) Provide government services electronically.

The government has launched UPI (Unified Payments Interface), the BHIM app, we have access to e-wallets like Pay TM and Free charge, and the newly launched Google Tez, which supports 7 regional languages. All these apps have 1 requirement - bank account.

The government should lower the barriers to having a bank account. India can only go cashless if 100% Indians have a bank account, otherwise, they would be dependent on currency notes for their day to day needs.

Joe said:

Hi all, Digitalization in country like India is a worth pondering concern. Everybody is aware what Mr. Arun Jaitley said that the primary motive of demonetization was to enhance digital use of money instead of paper Monnet; to some extent the motive was fulfilled. Digitalization has increased by 20-25% as per the statistics;however, the changes have been only seen in the urban or richer segment of population. The motive of highlighting this point is that we all know the literacy rate of India, in a country where 26.96% of total population is illiterate and where 21.9% of population is living below poverty line, how can we assume that going g totally cashless can help the economy. In spite, of being a developed country every year more than $10 million fraud occurs in US. There are nosceptic thoughts that Digitalization is a great way to increase economy but first we need to educate our people and we highly require a system to educate remote areas on Digitalization.

Neha said:

Everyone knows that the secondary motive of demonetisation to establish digital system and make India a digital India. The purpose got serve to the certain extent. Some of the report said that there is 22% increase in the digital transaction. There are different apps available for payment and Google is also launching an app called tez for the online payment. They are secure to the certain extent but there are hacker who can hack your account or digital system like ransom virus did. The main precaution is that the individual should avoided sharing their pin number and another confidential detail which can be used by hacker. So the digital payments are secure if an individual use it smartly and safely.

Ali Khan said:

Initially, I want to say that it is a prudent effort made by our government to go cashless.

It has many benefits as we all have considered before but what I want to convey are the hindrances that are creating a problem in such a well-intended effort.

Firstly, we all know the level of literacy of our country, no need to talk much.

Secondly, the crux is lack of awareness among people.

We are all living in a Global era of technology, but we should not forget every coin has 2 faces.

I want to highlight the grey one.

I think many of us k ow how many days are taken by the hackers to hack Windows no matter how much security is being offered by Microsoft.

Coming back to topic, I want to draw your attention towards hidden charges that one has to give which paying through cards.

There is a service charge of 2% for sweeping the card ones that means if you pay 1000 you will be charged an additional amount of 20 rs.

The Most important point I want to raise is that if anyone is cheated while digital payment it is difficult to recover the loss.

One of the reasons is that there is a cyber tribunal in Delhi for addressing such cases but unfortunately that judges are not appointed to the court since 2007, many won't believe it.

Someone can understand that how dreadful it will be for someone who met an unfortunate fraud.

So I want to say that before implementing cashless culture authorities should ensure proper resources to address the problems that are expected to come in the due course.

I want to conclude by saying that I am not a sceptic about the govt intention, but efforts should be made to ensure justice first.

Economics & Business

1. Is Foreign Direct Investment (FDI) in retail sector good for India?

Background

The cabinet decision on FDI in retail has triggered protests by opposition and key allies of the ruling United Progressive Alliance (UPA), who are demanding a roll back of the policy. The hour-long meeting held in Parliament House failed to resolve logjam in the two Houses as opposition parties, led by BJP and the left, stuck to their stand and demanded rollback of the Cabinet decision to allow 51 per cent FDI in multi- retail. Though at present only 53 cities with population not less than 10 lakhs in the country have been identified for FDI as the fourth-largest economy in the world in PPP terms, India is a preferred destination for FDI. During 2000-10, the country attracted $ 178 billion as FDI.

Favour

- This will bring modern technology to the country.
- Improve rural infrastructure. It would help build infrastructure and create a competitive market.
- Reduce wastage of agricultural produce.
- Enable our farmers to get better prices for their crops.
- Consumers will get commodities of daily use at reduced prices.
- Biggest beneficiary of this would be small farmers who would be able to improve productivity and realise higher remuneration by selling directly to large organised players and shorten the chain from farm to consumers.
- Government too stands to gain by this move through more transparent and accountable monitoring of goods and supply chain management systems. It can expect to receive an additional US $ 25-30 billion by way of taxes.

- Opening of retail can be seen as a solution for food inflation. Which has been confounding policy-makers? FDI in retail would help in building much needed back end infrastructure. Additionally, he said, investments in cold storage chain infrastructure would reduce loss of agriculture produce and provide more options to farmers.

Against

- Our interest rates today are as high as 14 percent to 16 per cent how do we compete with the economies which have a 4 per cent interest rate, Our infrastructure our trade facilities our labour laws, all these factors collectively don't make India low cost. So, do you want India to become a centre where we allow foreign companies to come in and set up these large chains which eventually instead of selling domestic products out sourcing internationally the cheapest sources and selling those products. Please remember domestic retail normally sources domestically. International retail sources internationally because they source from the cheapest sources.
- Even if big retail companies help the farmers in resurrecting their economy, what plan does the government has for millions of middlemen who are part of the business process chain that ensures manufactured products reach end users.
- We engage millions of uneducated and semi-educated people at various stages of retail business spread across towns and cities, but we are afraid that Tesco and Wal-Mart will only engage smart and educated workplace in small strength, comparatively.

Conclusion

- Government is taking this decision in good faith. Few persons and lobbies controlling the rates of food commodities in India. And bringing more competition in market will bring better prices for buyers as well as sellers of commodities. Parties protesting against FDIs in retail have choice to not allow FDIs in the states they are ruling. Government should make a regulatory body for the commodity trade as we have for cellular services.

2. HOW TO DEAL WITH HIGH OIL PRICES?

Currently we are facing a very serious issue, that is, hike in oil prices which is increasing rapidly. Now a day oil price is soaring the sky, which can be depicted as one of the major drawbacks in the growth of our economy because high oil prices generally cause a huge negative impact on the global economic growth and continuous depreciation of Indian rupees. So, we will discuss how to deal with high oil prices and the methods to overcome.

High oil prices cause a huge depreciation of economy

In India there is scarcity of natural resources due to which we must import petroleum from other countries. As day by day demand for petrol, oil products are increasing and consumption rate of oil being high, it consequently tends to increase in oil prices. Government is always blamed for ever increasing prices but somewhere we people are also responsible for high oil prices. It is our duty also to see how we can contribute towards reduction in oil prices. We must keep in mind that oil is not extracted in our country, so we should also preserve our resources and them in a sustainable manner.

According to my opinion only solution we are left with to deal with high oil prices is to reduce the consumption of oil i.e. Decrease in consumption = Decrease in demand = decrease in price.

Now the question arises how to reduce the consumption of oil? It can only be reduced by combined efforts of both government and Common People.

Following are the measures to be taken to reduce the consumption of oil which in turn will automatically tend to reduce the oil prices.

3. MULTINATIONAL CORPORATIONS: ARE THEY DEVILS IN DISGUISE?

Multinational companies cannot be a devil in disguise. They bring in revenue; provide job opportunities to thousands of people. It helps the country to get a global recognition. They undoubtedly work majorly to get profits.

However, it should not be forgotten that they bring quality to the services and raise the economy.

Most of the multinationals provides seamless services to employees like transport, accommodations, food, insurance, crèche etc.

The companies give high salaries to employees that keep them motivated. Few multinationals also provide future studies opportunities thereby assisting employees in their career.

They give onsite opportunities to people which helps them interacting with more people.

For some people, all that glitters are not gold! Few people think that they are devils in disguise because of the pressure and the work they expect from their employees.

This pressure leads to domestic issues, violence etc. no doubt they give high salary packages, but even take double the work from the employees.

Most of the multinational companies have clients from US and UK. Because of this the employees needs to manage two-time zones. This indeed leads to health disorders.

MNCs-Are they devils in disguise?

Well I must say that they are not devils in disguise from my perspective. If a country wants to get developed it requires FDI and for that we want MNC to enter our country. I know there are lot of criticisms regarding such, but it has more of advantages than disadvantages.

- MNCs bring advanced technologies along with themselves which we Indians never ever think in our life.
- It generates lot of employment opportunities and it lead to fall in unemployment rate of our country.
- It generates huge amount of revenue which we can use it in expanding our business in other countries in which we are superior to others.

- MNCs provide same product at cheap price as compared to our market and even of good quality.

Group Discussion- Multinational Corporations: Are they Devils in Disguise?

MNC also called as Multinational Corporation are not purely devil but they are surely not good for the country. As, more and more corporations are coming it looks like they are heading to rule any country they are in. They use us and get profits from our resources. They use our mind and talent to develop themselves and sustain in the corporate world. MNCs provide job to the people to promote their own product to the country they are in. MNCs are the root of all the cause of distress and instability in the country, because of them rich are getting richer and poor are getting poorer.

Group Discussion- MNC's: Are they devils in disguise?

Yes. They are so enormous in size that small producers and small businessman are suppressed beneath its size and they take away the job opportunities and India in the global market becomes mere a provider of the man workforce. They also have an influence on state policies; they arm with states making rules and regulation that suit them. MNC's are the biggest propagators of neo colonization.

General Interest

4. IS INDIA A SOFT NATION?

"Hard power yields obedience, while soft power yields acquiescence. The former is the foundation of state strength, but the latter helps consolidate that strength: History suggests that synergistic use of both forms of power allows a state to gain global influence".

India is a middle power. It does not belong to the major powers which command a subject role in international politics and make vital decisions about the fate and destiny of the international system. Nor is it, one of the minor powers which, with limited foreign policy autonomy, an object of the decisions of the major powers. In military capabilities, India's conventional capabilities are no match for those of the major powers, though it can boast of the third largest armed forces after China and the United States. Moreover, its capabilities for long range or rapid deployments are limited relative to the five major powers.

India, being a secular state has always faced difficulty in maintaining its integrity every now and then. But still, the unity among people and the prevailing brotherhood in the country have kept us intact despite being the most diversified country. We the people of India are basically very generous. We like our friends and, we love our enemies. Call it the teachings of Mahatma Gandhi or the modern form of Gandhigiri, compared to other nations, people in our country are not so rebellious. Our government always extends hands of friendship but never fastens its belt to initiate a war.

So far India has been labelled as a soft state. We have failed to protect our national interests on several occasions. Thanks to the petty politics and indecisiveness of our leadership, time and again our security forces have been the victim of apathy of our leadership. Imagine looking back fearfully each time you enter a temple, looking suspiciously at your fellow passengers while travelling by train. It is this reaction that a terrorist gloats on. To strike fear is the utmost target in his mind. When we succumb to that fear and terror, his goal is achieved. If, we show compassion for the accused, we will not achieve the goal of ridding our country of terrorism.

That is exactly what our problem is. We don't need to essentially prove that India is soft in combating terrorism. Anybody who reads newspapers will know that we are. Anybody who flies by Indian airways will know. Anybody who thinks that we gave a free ride to three of the worst criminals to a place called Kandahar in the distinguished company of our foreign minister would know that we are a soft state. The Indian Police have such a distinguished record of being a terror in UP. Our policemen rub chili powder into the eyes of prisoners. And if they do not sing as our policemen would want them to, they are hung upside down. Sadly, these brutalities are frequently committed in a country which is proud of its human rights awareness and constitutional guarantees. It's basically a matter of attitude. Our country's leaders' attitude does not reflect a national resolve to pay the price required to fight terrorism. That's our problem. Be it the Mumbai Attacks, or any other such blows, we have been passive in our approach to fight our enemies. There is no idea, why Kasab still seeks freedom even when video footages prove him guilty, and Indian Government has not taken any firm decision to fight this out.

We know that poverty in India still dominates prosperity. But, the glitter of IT and other prospering industries are praised to an extent that often covers the reality. We are no more in a situation to compare ourselves with China. We Indians still consider that China is a developing country like India (technically it is), but that is not true. The most powerful nation after US in terms of anything (especially military and defence) is China. Today's world currency markets are governed by China. US federal banks think twice before taking any decision regarding China, as it holds the maximum dollar reserves compared to any other country.

The nation can transcend only if there is peace, and it is the high time to terminate this nuisance of terrorism to their roots. Besides terrorism, India has numerous other problems too. The moment the country thinks of developing something it faces the tough reality. Building infrastructure is of immense importance for India but the pathetic condition of the poor gains priority. It is difficult must turn away from reality, high population, illiteracy, unemployment, social marginalization, poverty, highly appalling condition of public health and much more make our country weak.

In terms of population size, India is next only to China. But, population is both an asset and a curse for India. Its state of Uttar Pradesh (176 million) holds more population than that most of the major powers, Russia, UK (59 million), and France (59 million). India's middle class, which is estimated to be around 300 million and pool of scientific manpower which is the third largest in the world, is an asset, especially as all the major powers (barring China) are likely to depend on the Indian human resources because of their falling birth rates and ageing population. However, India's large numbers of unskilled and illiterate people are a bane for the country's power capability.

It is difficult to draw comparisons regarding soft power indicators as these are intangible. Soft power resources complement hard power resources and in the increasingly interdependent world, their importance as low cost means for exercising and preserving a state's power externally is becoming important. Major Powers use norms to legitimize their international status. In this regard, India's, normative influence has been reasonably high in the developing world. India has been a consistent voice on behalf of the developing countries.

As a leader of the non-aligned movement, it has championed global equality and new international economic order. This stance has been manifested in India's positions at the international trade talks and in the United Nations forums such as the UNCTAD. Further, India's own track record as a democracy also enhances its normative power. Major Powers use institutions to legitimize their position. In this context, India has been an active member of several international economic institutions and regimes. It has exercised institutional power from time to time, through its leadership in G-77, G-20 and the non-aligned group. It's contribution to the UN peacekeeping efforts since the early 1950s also enhance its institutional influence.

India, however, ranks low in other sources of soft power such as state capacity, strategy and- national leadership. Indian States has been unable to develop adequate strength to generate loyalty and discipline among its population. India is described as a 'soft state' also because of its failure to enforce enacted policies. In strategy and diplomacy, India's record has been mixed. While the anti-hegemonic theme of its diplomacy helped in establishing a role in the global institutions, forging third world solidarity and helped in bargain on North and South issues, it alienated the US and the Western countries, which attempted to contain and balance India by propping up a weaker Pakistan.

National leadership, important to translate other power resources into international influence, also has been a mixed bag. In the early years after independence, India's international influence has been mainly because of the commanding leadership of Jawaharlal Nehru. Though India became inward looking after the reverses in the 1962 Sino India war, Mrs. Indira Gandhi did exert some influence overseas.

Through its independent existence, India has largely been a soft state committed to rising through a non-militaristic foreign policy. It has sought to propound principles of peaceful co-existence, only to find these rebuffed by more pragmatic neighbours. Between 1947 and 1964, the Nehru Doctrine cost India sovereignty over Pakistan occupied Kashmir and suzerainty over Tibet. With its deep faith in the binding nature of gentlemen's agreements and international law, it also left India open to betrayals such as 1962.

The Chinese invasion of 1962 and Pakistani invasion of 1965 led to a stronger emphasis on hard power. Under the Indira Doctrine (late 196Os-80s), New Delhi set out to establish India as the South Asian hegemon. Indian forces speedily repulsed an opportunistic Chinese probe in 1967 and paid Pakistan back for its past transgressions in 1971. The more confrontational tone of Indian security policy however, caused disquiet in foreign capitals, prompting some Western and Arab states, as well as China, to bandwagon with Pakistan.

The Indira Doctrine demonstrated the limits of what hard power could achieve by it. Despite the best efforts of New Delhi, extra-regional forces intervened in South Asian affairs, to India's detriment. From the 1970s onwards, China provided extensive help to the Pakistani nuclear programme. The Soviet Union occupied Afghanistan in 1979, prompting the United States enter a covert alliance with Pakistan. During the 1980s, a convergence of these two vectors (acquisition of nuclear weapons and growing expertise in covert action), provided Islamabad with the means and self-confidence to launch a proxy war against India.

End-route to becoming a superpower, India shall at some point have to consider partially shedding its soft image to earn the respect due to a strong nation. Hitherto, its strategic restraint against Pakistan-based terrorists has been lauded by foreign governments. Such praise however, has also restricted India's policy options – a situation which is now starting to show diminishing returns, as strategic experts overseas question whether India can ever demonstrate the muscle and the will needed to qualify as a real super power. India needs to develop a politically, diplomatically and operationally sustainable response to cross-border terrorism. It needs to balance multiple considerations, such as protecting its citizens from terrorist attacks, promoting secularism domestically, preserving international goodwill and strengthening peace lobbies in Pakistan. Within these parameters, the order of priorities must be understood – the safety of Indian nationals and the preservation of domestic stability through secularism come first. Achieving these higher priorities without prejudice to the other two may require exemplary yet covert use of force against Pakistan-based terrorists.

Counter-terrorism experience of Western democracies suggests that decapitation strikes can greatly damage terrorist groups psychologically as well as operationally. For instance: in May 1980, Arab terrorists occupied the Iranian embassy in London, taking several hostages. After initially attempting to negotiate, the British government ordered Special Forces to storm the building. What happened next was controversial as eyewitnesses say that once the hostages were freed, the rescue force killed the terrorists in cold blood. Although hard evidence of a 'no-prisoners' directive never surfaced, media speculation was rife. Apparently, such speculation itself acted as a deterrent-no further incidents of political hostage taking occurred in Britain.

India should adopt a comparable approach to foreign-based terrorists: one of 'silent signalling'. Indian Special Forces should relentlessly eliminate terrorists in their safe havens, even as New Delhi pursues symbolic peace talks with Islamabad. To become a superpower, India needs to project a benign international image without being weak or indecisive vis-a-vis an insignificant adversary such as Pakistan. The latter has already been labelled by a 2008, United States Army report as being at risk of state failure. Instead of attracting international hostility and further destabilizing the already weak Pakistani state through a military offensive (although that remains an option if all else fails), India should first try fighting cross-border terrorists through covert usage of hard power.

As independent India seeks to establish itself in the global arena, it needs to learn the lessons of history and exploit the benefits of both kinds of power. The examples of authoritarian states such as the Soviet Union and Maoist China suggest that open and unrestrained use of hard power triggers the formation of a balancing coalition against a rising state. At the same time, no country has ever gained international respect just for being peace-loving and projecting a benign image of itself. Preserving the goodwill currently generated by Indian soft power while retaining the strategic autonomy provided by hard power is therefore, a key challenge for New Delhi. This is especially true of relations with Pakistan. To fight terror, the country needs to strengthen its security and intelligence. The need of hour is to revamp border security, maritime security and aerial security. The nation needs a complete recast of its intelligence mechanism. There is a pressing need for stringent counter-terrorism policy and its implementation. To weed out terrorism from its roots, India needs to terrorize the terrorists and their sympathizers. Sooner the leadership recognizes this; the better it is for the nation.

5. SHOULD RESEARCH ON HUMAN CLONING BE BANNED?

Cloning is defined as a form of genetic engineering in which the DNA of a person, animal, plant, or even a bacterium is used to produce a perfect or near –perfect genetic replica of the original.

Abolishing human cloning before it begins, has been a controversial debate since the 1940's. Many researchers believe that, regardless of whether a law is passed to eliminate cloning research or not, human cloning will eventually become a reality because it is an inevitable consequence of scientific advancement. The controversy raises fundamental questions about how technology affects our lives and the consequences we will face in the future. Who will be cloned and why? Are humans playing God for a living? Is cloning a safe procedure? This essay will elaborate on reasons why human cloning should be prohibited before it begins.

Bringing back the deceased is said to be the most common motivation cited by those interested in human cloning. The growing numbers of people who desire to clone a lost husband, wives, child, or relative is steadily growing. The idea that the clone of a dead person will be a complete replica of that person is a misconception. As those familiar with the technology often point out, cloning a person will duplicate only his or her physical appearance and other genetic elements, not the person's personality and memories. "Even if humans were cloned, they would merely look like each other, not be exact copies in fact, twins are more alike than clones would be". The biological reason for this is that the clone's cells would have mitochondria from the egg donor, rather than the nucleus donor. Clones would only become an appearance substitute with a mind of their own. If a grieving family decides to clone a deceased family member and the genetic clone is wicked and malicious, what will the family do? Should they "exchange" it for another clot...?

EDUCATION

6. ADVANTAGES OF CO-EDUCATION

Co-education is a system where both the genders (male and female) participate in a same learning centre or an educational institution. In this process, both the genders would benefit equally in learning or attaining knowledge from the institution and each other. This method of education even though is becoming common all over the world, there are still few parts of the country who feel sometimes segregation is for the betterment of the learning process. However, there are same amount of group who feels, segregation of the genders causes trouble to the learning process and makes it more complicated.

Let us now look at some of the co-education advantages and disadvantages.

A good education system is said to be progressive only if it respects both the genders and giving the same education under a single roof. Co-education institutions help in laying the foundation for both the genders to learn how to co-exist with respect and dignity.A co-Edu.schools' advantages for both the gender, are many.Here are the few points that explain the advantages of co-education system.

1. Develops mutual respect:

Co-education allows both the genders to mingle with each other and to know how to co-exist with respect. By this process of getting mingled under one learning institution, they develop mutual understanding towards each other. And there is no place of hesitation2 or partiality among the genders when it comes to performing activities like cultural, academics or sports. People get to know how to respect each other and their emotional level. You get to know each other's strengths and weaknesses and develop the ability to accept them as they are.

2. Helps to overcome the fear of opposite gender:

In general, there are lot of differences in behaviour of both the genders which brings in fear and hesitance in striking a conversation, this fear can be for a boy or a girl. This kind of shyness, hesitation or fear can be overcome when they are put up in a co-education system where they will be compelled to talk and create a friendly environment where there is no fear. It is very natural phenomenon where both the genders must be together to face the world, your senior could be a male or a female and you would have to create a friendly environment and are at ease with the opposite sex. Hence, co-education would help them to know the opposite sex better creating a comfort zone where the communication is easier.

3. Healthy competition:

Competition is always an essential part in any kind of challenges in life be it personal or professional. And especially in education it is good to have a healthy competition among the peers which lets you learn how to cope with your failures early in life no matter who the winner is. When it comes to opposite genders it would be more competitive because of your ego, and this is one good way to improve the personal standards so that you don't get personal on every failure and are able to face it with dignity. So, co-education systems in nurtures challenges among the opposite genders in a healthy way that helps you to maintain your dignity and educates you to face your failures and learn from them rather than turn them into revengeful act.

4. Develops self-esteem among the genders:

Self-esteem is very essential and must be built in good way and the best place to start with it is the learning institutions where you can face all types of personality early in your life. Co-education learning centres help to lay the early foundation for maintaining dignity and self-esteem. Many institutions give extra attention to students who feel that they are less worthy than the others and offer counselling sessions that help in building up their personality and making them stronger to face the world. Co-education helps both the genders to respect each other's self-esteem and build a confidence about their own self helping them to step out in the open without feeling intimidated.

5. Encourages the survival in future:

Survival in future for any of the gender in today's world can happen only when we learn to co-exist. From working together to making a marriage successful is all about team work and the effort given by both male and female. Team building activities in early stages help both the genders to learn how to co-exist and this can only be provided in the co-educational system. By this way, co-education is an essential part in education system which pushes the genders to work together and blend with each other to survive in this brutal world.

6. Character enhancement:

A recent study reveals that children tend to behave very decently in a civilised manner in the presence of other gender provided they have been in this scenario for long. This is very essential in an institution setup as well as it will have a huge impact in their personal front for the people of opposite sex to behave well with each other. Hence, co-education plays an important role in character building. They emphasize on the fact that they have to respect and listen to the opposite sex as they listen and respect one from their own.

7. No space for discrimination:

Quarrel among the peers is very common be it at home, workplace or educational institutions. This may happen due to no proper understanding, misconceptions, miss-communications, uncomfortable, no respect for other sex and ignorance. We hear a lot of news that comes on the internet, newspapers and television about how the genders are abusing each other at workplace or at home and this can only be improved when there is a good understanding between the two. This is very much reduced in a co-education system as they understand better each other and hence, reducing the bad behaviour and harsh reactions from each other. So, co-education system reduces any kind of discrimination and increases respect towards the opposite sex.

8. Resource handling:

Be it any country there will be a shortage of lecturers for knowledge if there are separate institutions or centres right from school to college as there would be huge demand for teachers which might not be possible to fill in. And it also breeds monetary loss to the government or a private institution when they invest huge amount for separate lecturers teaching the same thing to students across institutions. Hence, co-education system has an advantage of proper resource handling.

9. Promotes a controlled environment:

When both the genders are put up in same environment, there are more possibilities of following good ethics, disciplined use of language, and proper dressing etc. You would know what the needs are of the opposite sex and how they behave helping you to avoid unfavourable situations. Co-education supports good decent environment with more value-based education emphasising on respect and love for each other.

DISADVANTAGES OF A CO-EDUCATION SYSTEM

Every establishment has pros as well as cons and hence we need to look at every angle before we decide in which direction we must go. Even though there are many advantages of having a co-education system, our society still puts forward few inhibitions which do not accept the concept. Here are few disadvantages which is commonly expressed about co-education system. They are,

1. Chances of distractions could be more:

Teenage is a very dangerous phase in anybody's life. It is very common among the teens to undergo psychological changes when they are in company of the other gender and feel attracted towards them. And especially at crucial stage where they are in a process of defining their career path, it could cause lot of distractions and might disturb their knowledge gain period. Hence, parents often wonder if co-education institutions would be right choice for your kin to learn and whether they should avoid co-education system.

2. Unethical activities:

Crimes have become common when both the genders are put up in the same education environment. There might be lot characteristic changes among boys and girls. When they mismatch, some ferocious kids tend to commit various harassments, physical toughness, and emotional stress to people around. The weaker lot can suffer at the hands of the opposite sex pushing them into depression and other psychological problems. Hence, people hesitate to support co-education system to ensure that their kids are in a safe environment and this is especially for the girls.

3. More involvement in personal feelings:

As the saying goes, opposite things attract each other, it applies to the humanly world also. Attractions among the opposite genders are the most commonly used excuse to avoid co-education system. It is natural to get physically attracted to the other gender at a crucial age of life where curiosity takes over your heart. So, parents feel co-education is a risky task to take forward as they can have an easy access to distractions within the institutions. An emotional involvement at an early stage can come with lot baggage that can force a child to deviate from their goals.

4. Unwanted arguments and issues can create an unhealthy environment:

Both the genders come from different school of thought and hence contradiction of thoughts is common among boys and girls. If the arguments are not handled in a proper behaviour then it can sometimes might lead to unwanted arguments and might divert from their studies. It can lead to lot of complaints and parents making the rounds at the school for the improper behaviour from their kin.

This will also make the teachers get troubled a lot because of their behaviour and an irritated teacher can never give their 100% towards teaching. This is what worries any parent when they come to know that the issues in the school are costing his or her kin's studies and hence pushing them to select a convent rather than co-educational institutions.

5. Reduces the options for schools or colleges for the genders:

With schools and colleges dedicated towards a single gender, creates a lot of shortage for the opposite genders to apply. If the demand for teachers increases then the demand for institutions based on gender also increases. Establishing an institution is an expensive affair which may not be a feasible option to implement all over the world. There can be a scenario where you have more supply of students but less number of institutions to work with it. Dedicated institutions can also lead to lot of discomfort in handling the other gender when it comes to working in a professional world creating issues in your career path and growth.

There are both advantages as well as disadvantages for any kind of education system including co-education system. The real good social environment will nurture positives of the society and help in dealing with the negatives in a dignified manner. There is no educational system in the world that has eradicated the negatives of the society but a co-educational system can definitely work towards mending the gap between the genders and building a bridge of friendship. In this promising era of empowerment, it is very essential to have a co-education system to fit the survival of environment where both the genders have their place and say. It is now important to incorporate early in life to respect and love the opposite gender to help build a beautiful world of peace.

7. Examinations – has it killed education

As we know that the examination system has come to be the main theme of modern education. Everyone from his early child-hood should take endless examinations and succeed in passing them, before he could graduate from a college or university. As much importance has been attached to it in school education, it has been subjected to mounting criticism as to its validity. People in favour of it praise this system to great extent; and those opposing to it maintain that such a system should be abolished. A lot of people think that the examination system should be abolished. In the first place, because of the existence of the examination system, students go out for gaining high marks so that they often forget the main purpose of education. Many so-called "clever" students are nothing but bookworms who merely know the skeleton of knowledge. The aim of education is to enable stu-dents to learn how to live, how to work, and how to contribute to the country with their expertise. To do this, the students must receive training, in physical as well as mental areas. But the present examination system has discouraged students from making such an attempt. Furthermore, since the students try so hard to memorize, in a short period of time, as much as possible, psychologically, they will forget the whole subject as soon as the exam is over. Surely, this is one of the greatest wastes ever made in the history of hu-man civilization. I do have the same opinions as those people do. But I do not agree with them that the examination system should be abolished. Let's clarify some things first. Take Thomas Edison and Marie Curie for instance. Edison stayed at school for only three months when he was young. Because he always asked strange questions that his teachers thought he was a fool. So they sent him away from school. Little poor Tom had to teach himself to learn but he made more than 2,000 inventions years later. Marie Curie went to Paris to...

8. How effective are Indian B-schools?

Indian Government has liberalized business education in 1990s, resulting in rapid growth of Management Institutes offering the programmes both at graduate & undergraduate levels. Indian management education is almost a replica of US Business education particularly in the area of pedagogy, curricula, industry interface & academic research models, but it is observed that Indian management institutes are struggling hard to introduce several adaptations because of differences in the work culture system. Owing to globalization lot of changes are noticed in the functioning of industries across the world requiring having the manpower with multi-skills rather than simply knowledge oriented. Top Management institutes are continuously changing the contents & delivery modes. On this back ground it is equally important to address the various issues & concerns of Indian management education experiencing with time. This purpose of this case study is to engage all concerned in a serious discussion with a view to revamping management education in India as a prelude to better participation and viability in the global economy. This paper examines the issues that need to be addressed and a possible direction so that management education can be rejuvenated.

Education had been lately turned into more of a business than an effort to educate the people of the country. There are private universities spread across the country and most of them would provide management degrees. It has become such a business that every rich man today wants to open up a B-school and offer numerous seats to lure in students. With the value of a professional degree like MBA, it was the ultimate end of a shift from the world of education to a professional life. It seemed as a final sign-off to education. One having good scores in a MBA degree was sure to get placed in a good company with a good pay back. Such was the efficiency and the importance of the degree. But recently the number of colleges providing this degree had brought down the importance of the course. Every other college is offering a MBA degree. This is creating a weak base for the students to succeed in this transition. On the academic floor, the MBA Programme was once supreme. It is a dramatic scenario but not an unexpected one. With the growing popularity of the course which actually marked its downfall, many more will be closing down in the coming months. These institutes no longer see business sense in offering an MBA course, preferring to use the land for more lucrative ventures. As S. S. Mantha, chairman of the All-India Council for Technical Education, puts it, "Colleges in remote India and institutes of poor quality are not getting students." Will it again help the course to nullify the current changes and get back to where it actually stood or will it be a mark that the importance of it is degrading? Policies: Diminishing quality in teaching is one prime factor attributed to this decline of education standard in India. There is also lack of meaningful research in the Indian colleges and universities. The government has imposed restrictions on the universities in the matter of fee structures and the compensation to highly performing teachers. To develop a better research institute requires high quality professors, who are highly paid. But in India, there are no mechanisms in place to ensure that highly performing professors are well rewarded. This is the important reason for the migration of highly qualified professors to developed countries. Until and unless the AICTE takes it job seriously and does a bit of study in the state and plug the holes in the system

Current Topics

- Ban 500, 1000 notes - Corruption Uprooted or just changing clothes!
- Can we dream of hosting the Olympics?
- Chinese Goods vs Indian Goods
- Do we really need Smart Cities?
- Economic growth is more important than Ecological protection
- EQ or IQ
- Extra curricular activities should be made compulsory in school
- Face book needs to clarify policies on content removal!
- How demonetization is affecting common people more than black money holders?
- How is Technology impacting the Banking sector?
- Is compulsory attendance really needed in college?
- Is it fair to spare political parties from income tax investigation?
- Is the youth of India confident or confused?
- Non-execution of GST bill might herald end of present government
- One India One Election - Pros and Cons
- PM's vision to make India a Manufacturing Hub - dream or a practical possibility?
- Polythene bags must be banned!
- Problems unite us, Religion divides us
- Should Hindi be the official language of India?
- Should national anthem be played in cinema halls?
- Should we change the present system of education in our country?
- Solution of corruption is a mirage till we catch top public figure
- Will Reliance Jio be a sustainable business model in a country like India?
- Youth in Politics

Economics & Business

- Are Indians Less Quality Conscious?
- Ethics in Business are just a Passing Fad
- Is the Consumer really the King in India?
- Commercialization of Health Care: Good or Bad?
- Is there any Point in having a Business Strategy when the World changes from Month to Month?
- Is the Patents Bill Good for India?
- Is the Business of Business only Business?
- Public Sector being a Guarantor of Job Security is a Myth
- Capitalism is a very Flawed System but the others are so much worse
- How can a Business get rid of the Bad Name that it has earned?
- Government Pumping Money into the Economy is not the Solution for our Economic Problems
- Is the Budgeting Exercise of any Use?
- Should Agricultural Subsidies be stopped?
- Is MNCs Superior to Indian Companies?
- Advertising is a Waste of Resources
- P rivatization will lead to Less Corruption
- Should India break Diplomatic Ties with Pakistan?
- Use of Force by Banks to Recover Loans
- Skilled Manpower Shortage in India
- Technology Creates Income Disparities
- In our economic matters, there is an excessive tendency towards the thinking rather than doing.
- Every cloud has a silver lining
- Is disinvestment really that good for India or is a rethink in order?
- Are co-operatives relevant in today's globalised environment?
- Foreign aid is a dangerous drug that can stimulate in small doses but become fatally addictive in larger doses.
- Government should clean its own hands before pointing finger at the private sector for corruption.
- Reforms have to grow up.
- Globalization vs. Nationalism
- Economic freedom not old fashioned theories of development will lead to growth and prosperity
- Should businessmen run the finance ministry?

- Should important services like transport be left to market forces?.
- Who says MNCs are superior to Indian companies?
- What we need to reduce scams is better regulatory bodies.
- Trade can help the poor?
- Water resources should be nationalised
- Are Co-operatives Relevant in Today's Global Environment?
- Indian villages - our strength or our weakness?
- Space Missions are a Wastage of Resources for a Resource-Starved Nation like India
- Satyam Scandal would Impact Foreign Investments in India
- Private Participation in Infrastructure is Highly Desirable
- Developing Countries need Trade, not Aid
- Poverty in Third World Countries is due to Prosperity in First World Countries
- Indian Economy: Old Wine in New Bottle!
- Is Globalization Really Necessary?
- What shall we do about our Ever-Increasing Population?
- Banning of Trade Unions will be Beneficial in Growth of the Economy
- Why can't India be a World-Class Player in Manufacturing Industry as it is in IT & BPO Sectors?
- We Need Drinking Water and Not Coke & Pepsi in Rural India
- Rise of Regional Blocs Threatens Independent Nations like India
- Should the public sector be privatized?

General Interest

- Should Sting Operations be Carried Out?
- Nuclear War cannot be won and should not be fought
- Is Swapping Terrorists for Hostages an Encouragement to Plane-Hijackers?
- Brain-Drain has to be stopped
- Doctors' Accountability to Improve Health-Care
- Universal Disarmament is a Must
- Is India Aping the Western Obsession with Celebrities?
- India at 60: A Senior Citizen?
- Unrest in Countries around India
- Flexi Timings or Fixed Timings - Which is better at Work?

- Individual Brilliance Certainly makes a Difference
- Is Paperless Office a Reality or Not?
- Rules & Regulation Breed Corruption
- Do NGOs in India Really Work for Others OR Work for their Own Vested Interests?
- Science Is A Boon Or Bane
- Should Animals be used for Testing New Drugs & Medical Procedures?
- Security Cameras & Privacy
- Advertisements Cheat People, Hence Should Be Banned
- Borderless World: A Threat?
- Borderless World: A Myth or Reality?
- Secularism has become a Tool to Justify the Wrongs done by the Minorities
- What is the Difference between People who do Things Rightly and People who do Right Things?
- Corruption is a Necessary Evil for Success in Any Sphere
- Beauty Pageants are a Must
- How to Deal with International Terrorism?
- Are Peace and Non-Violence Outdated Concepts?
- Indian Army as a Career Option
- Capital Punishment should be Banned or Allowed?
- Is Dependence on Computers a Good Thing?

Management Topics

- We Need More Entrepreneurs than Managers
- Rise in MBA Salaries is Not Sustainable in the Long Run
- Can One Contribute to the Social Sector while Being Employed in the Corporate World?
- The Rush for MBA is really a Rush for Big Money
- Will Mumbai's Film Industry ever evolve into a Truly Modern Corporative One?
- Indians Perform Better as Individuals than in Groups/Teams
- Positive Attitude and not Knowledge is required for Business Success
- Are Ethics just Business Pretence?
- Ethics in Business are just a passing fashion
- Is an MBA necessary to succeed in life?
- Family owned business vs. professionally run businesses

- Smaller businesses and start-ups have more scope for professional growth.
- Dot com or doubt com?
- Managerial skills learnt in the classroom can never match those learnt from experience
- Management Education in India
- Is Leaders Born or are they made in Business Schools?
- Is Management an Art or a Science?
- The objective of Management is to maximize profits
- Should GD be Part of Campus Placements?
- Role of Ethics in Business
- Is Management Education Required for Business?
- Whether Hard-Working or Smart-Working is Desirable?
- Women are better at Multi-Tasking
- Does Morality have an Essence in Corporate Life?
- Retention of Employees
- Do Women make Good Managers?
- Celebrity Brand Endorsement: Effective Advertising?
- The Salaries that MBAs Get is more than they deserve
- Engineering Students are wasting their Time in Management Studies; they have Another Way to go
- MBA in India is highly Over-rated

Creative Topics

- A Ship Docked in Harbour cannot face the Storms
- Do Beauty and Brains Go Together?
- Every Cloud has a Silver Lining
- Rules are Meant to be Broken
- Food Comes First, Ethics Later
- Let Sleeping Dogs Lie
- There is No Right Way of Doing the Wrong Thing
- Is Love Precious or Poisonous?
- Is God Male?
- Good Things Always Come from Good Thinking
- In Today's World, Everything is Uncertain except Death & Taxes
- Men are from Mars; Women are from Venus
- Cleanliness is a Fundamental Responsibility of an Indian Citizen
- A Person should not be too honest; Straight Trees are cut first

- Nice Guys Finish Last
- All Work and No Play Makes Jack a Dull Boy
- The Wheel is Turning Round and Round
- If I was the Finance Minister/Prime Minister
- Group Task: How can we have Mount Everest in India?
- When I woke up in the morning I saw?
- Up the Down Staircase
- Just as we have smoke free zones, we should have child free zones
- The Nostradamus Code: World War III

Social Topics

- Terrorism in India
- Religion should not be mixed with politics
- Should Smoking be Banned Completely?
- Effects of Television on Youth
- Love Marriages Vs Arranged Marriages
- Are beauty contests degrading womanhood?
- Films are corrupting the Indian Youth
- Morals & Values among Indians is Degenerating
- Censorship in Movies & Our Culture
- Foreign Television Channels are Destroying Our Culture
- With Media Publishing and Telecasting Trivia, Censorship is the Need of the Hour
- Women are not fit for Defence Services
- Women Empowerment - A Cause for Increasing Divorce Rate in India
- Showing Violence and Crimes should not be allowed in films and on television.
- Classical Music Heritage and the Growing Pop-Culture
- Individual Freedom and Civil Society
- Influence of Online Social Networks on our Youth
- Is Remixing Good Trend in Music?
- Bride burning and dowry may look bad, but are an integral part of India.
- Our Culture is Decaying
- We are not serious about saving Wildlife/Environment
- The education system needs serious reforms
- The Internet is an exercise in hype
- Marriage is a social trap

Politics

- Should voters be given a NOTA (None of the Above) choice?
- Is our Political System Reason for our Backwardness?
- Educational qualification for Politicians
- Necessity of Women Quota Bill for Women Empowerment
- Voters, not Political Parties, are Responsible for the Criminalization of Politics
- Should We Pursue our Policy of Dialogue with Pakistan?
- The Way Forward for India is to Join Hands with Pakistan on Nuclear Matters
- Need for Good Leaders in India
- Politics is run by the Barrel of Gun
- Retirement Age for Politicians
- Corruption is the Price we pay for Democracy
- What India needs is a Dictatorship?
- Value-based Politics is the Need of the Hour
- Religion should not be mixed with Politics
- Democracy is Hampering India's Progress
- Should Tainted Ministers Allowed to Contest Elections?
- Presidential v/s Parliamentary Form of Government in India
- Reservations in the Private Sector
- Decreasing defence expenditure and increasing social expenditure is the need of the hour
- India should go for the presidential form of democracy

Sports

- If Winning isn't everything, why do they Keep the Score?
- Cricket in India has lost its Sheen
- Is T20 Cricket killing Real Cricketing Skills?
- Six Billion and One Bronze!
- Are Cricketers to be blamed for Match Fixing?
- Modern Day Sport in Industrialized Society is an Industry
- Cricket as a National Obsession is a Detriment to Other Sports

Education: -

- Do we really Need Education to be Successful?
- Government Control in Higher Education is Interfering and Not Required
- Privatization of Higher Education

- Should the Government Set-up More IITs and IIMs, OR should it be use the Money for Primary & Secondary Education?
- Foreign Universities in India
- E-Learning: A Substitute for Classroom Learning?
- Is Reservation in Higher Education Only Alternative for Social Equality?
- Private Educational Institutions: Good or Bad
- Should Management Education be subsidized?

TOP TIPS FOR YOUR TECH INTERVIEW

You've landed the interview — great job! Whether you are diving into the job hunt for the first time or returning to the drawing board after years as a developer, tech interviews can still seem incredibly daunting. You have put in all of the hard work, but the uncertainty of the process can make even seasoned professionals nervous. But with the right preparation and approach, you can spend less time worrying and more time impressing. Check out the following tips to help your skills shine.

BEFORE THE INTERVIEW

Do Your Research

A little bit of research can go a long way when it comes to prepping for your interview? Look up the company on Glass door, and if you know the name of your interviewer, research them on LinkedIn ahead of time. Knowing whether your interviewer is an HR manager, a project lead, or a senior developer will help you set better expectations for what kinds of questions will be asked. Researching the types of questions that may come up can go a long way as well. Check out Geek Interview to explore a database of interview questions categorized by specific roles.

Practice Makes Perfect

Live coding and technical testing are often key components of the technical interview process. Practicing timed and uncertain questions can help you nail this segment on interview day. Check out LeetCodeto explores a bank of practice coding interview questions and Hacker Rank to complete a range of timed challenges. Consider getting up in front of a whiteboard and having a friend ask you some questions, as you may be asked to do some live coding during the interview. Practicing all scenarios will help you get comfortable with whatever might be thrown your way.

Polish Your Portfolio

Having a great portfolio of projects that demonstrate your skills will go a long way in convincing an employer that you know your stuff. Projects should demonstrate marketable skills and highlight your abilities in the languages required in the position you are interviewing for. Additionally, projects should demonstrate complexity, including 3-5 distinct features. These can include things like integrating with an API, interacting with a database, or having a login or authentication component. Consider using a framework such as Angular or React for front end sites and projects. The number of projects you have is not nearly as important as the complexity and professionalism of any given project. Having your portfolio organised and easily accessible will help make a great impression with your interviewer.

DURING THE INTERVIEW

Take a Pause

When the interviewer asks a question, whether technical or not, take a moment to think and consider your answer before beginning a response. Particularly for tricky technical problems, taking a pause shows depth of thought. If you feel the need to answer immediately, throw out a filler phrase like "That's a great question" or repeating the question to give yourself time to think.

Break It Down

When it comes to technical questions, employers often are as interested in your thought process as they are in your final answer. Don't assume any knowledge (unless your interviewer says to) and articulate every step of your thought process. This will help make your answer clear and keep you on track.

Confidence Is Key

Even if you are uncertain in an answer, put your best foot forward when solving a problem. Avoid self-deprecating humor...giving yourself the benefit of the doubt will make your interviewer more likely to do that same.

Ask Questions

This advice applies both during and after the interview. If you are unsure about a question, ask clarifying questions to ensure you are zoning in on the right things. Additionally, ask questions of your interviewer after the interview to highlight your depth of knowledge and interest in the company and the opportunity. For technical roles, showing an interest and knowledge in technical team dynamics will help contribute to your credibility. Consider asking questions about scrum, agile, team dynamics, and current/future projects to demonstrate your willingness to be a team player.

AFTER THE INTERVIEW

Follow Up

Be sure to send a thank-you note to your interviewer(s) after the interview. Generally, you can send this note via email, but make sure to tailor it specifically to topics from the interview, including ideas you may have for improving the company's site, or further examples of work you highlighted in the interview.

Bonus Tip

No matter the outcome, every interview is a learning opportunity. If you find certain questions tripping you up, take note, look-up answers after the interview, and keep practicing similar problems to be better prepared for you next opportunity!

5

Important Group Discussion Topics for SBI PO

As of now, you know the importance of the 3rd stage of the selection process. So to help you & get selected in SBI PO we are providing you with 40 Important Group Discussion topics for SBI PO you should practise.

1. Is right to freedom being misused?

Now, we are coming to the question. First we need to define 'misuse'.

Incitement of Violence: If a person, by his speech, incites a crowd to commit violence against a person or group of persons, he/she cannot claim that this was his right to free speech.

Sedition: I have strong issues with the wording of this law which imposes restrictions even on legitimate anti-government speech and harmless criticism. Nevertheless, the courts have interpreted it now, to mean include only the speech which calls for violence against the Indian State under seditious speech. It also includes, speech which threatens to jeopardize our relations with friendly countries.

DEFAMATION

Contempt of court

Apart from this, everything should be fair game. If you consider, any speech which shocks, disgusts or offends your sensibilities as 'misuse', then you are missing the whole point of the Right.

To answer, your question: The people, who did misuse the right are in jail. The people who are being accused of misusing the right are only using it. You cannot prosecute them just for having an opinion.

All said, that does not mean you cannot criticize them and discourage them. That is your right to free speech.

2. Cleanliness should be the fundamental duty of every citizen.

Cleanliness is next to godliness. The main problem of our country is illiteracy, if people are educated then they show there footmarks on every walk of their life. What I mean to tell that our government should take serious initiative to eradicate this problem and highlight problems related to untidy environment to general public.

Most of the developing nations are spending crores of money in recycling waste and they are regularly improving to stop wastage and educating people towards their attitudes. We should always be aware about the untidiness around us. We should teach the people around us to keep our surroundings clean and tidy. Cleanliness is necessary for an individual. It leads to a country's progress. For example, if one is suffering from any ailment resulted from un-cleanliness; one is not capable to concentrate in his/her work (especially studying). So it results in reduction in the knowledge that will be gained if an individual is healthy. Every individual's knowledge and experience even gives uplift to economically down-trodden people those results in country's progress as a whole.

We the citizens of India are having the utmost responsibility of keeping the govt properties with clean and godliness.

In Hyderabad the citizens have the habit of chewing the pan and ghutka and the habit of spitting on the roads and important walls if you go to the historic charminar the side walls of full of spittoons. Though there are strict warnings mentioned, the visitors damn care for it as they are illiterate over the issue.

I suggest maximum punishment to those who deface the walls with posters and paint the walls with pan marks.

3. What are the merits and de-merits of One Rank One Pension scheme?

One Rank One Pension (OROP) is a scheme in which every eligible candidate retiring in a particular rank gets the same pension, irrespective of his date of retirement. Till now, soldiers who retired more recently receive more pension than those who retired earlier because pensions are dependent on last salary received and successive pay commissions have raised salaries.

Advantages:

This scheme is a compensation for early retirement and is a national obligation.

Soldiers have short careers because jawans usually retire at the age of 35 years whereas a civilian retires at 60. To make up for the shorter working lives of these soldiers, they need compensation that is comparable to what a soldier of same rank retiring today would get from the government. Lt. Gen Raj Kadyan (Chairman of Indian Ex-Servicemen Movement) says, "The stark difference can be seen after the implementation of the Sixth Pay Commission. For equal service, a Sepoy who retired prior to 1996 gets 82% lower pension than a Sepoy who retires after 2006. Similarly, among officers, a pre-1996 Major gets 53% lower pension than his post 2006 counterpart." The government has announced this revised benefit along with arrears under OROP scheme to more than 2 lakh pensioners.

Disadvantages:

- Due to the increase in the defense pension budget, the current liability will increase from Rs. 60,238 crore to Rs. 64959.34 crore i.e. an increase of Rs. 4721.34 for the financial year 2015–16.
- Often it happens that people who retire in the same rank earn different pensions because they have served for a longer time in that rank. For example: A Colonel who served for 12 years earns more than the Colonel who served for only 4 years in the same rank. Equating their pensions was unlikely to withstand a legal challenge.
- The government is also afraid that there might be a similar demand from the civilian pensioners in the near future and hence, the public pressure would be very difficult to handle.

Considering the cost of living / price index and inflation, had there been a fair / transparent mechanism set in place, this demand / expectation would not have been there. The soldiers (Non Officers) retire at a very young age, and justifiably need to be taken care of. Officers rarely have the chance of a second career and the bulk retires at the rank of a Colonel which is 54 yrs. There is definitely a need to look into these aspects, otherwise the Defence forces will further fall from the present low level as the choice of a young man / woman's career. And you will see a further degradation in the quality of intake. At the same time, the BSF, CRPF, ITBP and other para military forces will follow suit, with similar demands. And the Indian coffers are not so comfortable to withstand these pressures, thanks to our Political muck, lack of policies, lack of vision and corruption.

I would like to draw your attention to what American President Barack Obama has said— "So long as I am Commander-in-Chief, we will sustain the strongest military the world has ever known. When you take off the uniform, we will serve you as well as you've served us - because no one who fights for this country should have to fight for a job, or a roof over their head, or the care that they need when they come home."

Recently I travelled to the US. At the Indian airport (T-3, Delhi), prior to boarding the United Airlines Flight, the crew (All Indian) started organising the boarding they announced that all US military personnel, serving or retired may please board first.

Now, I know that some of you will scoff at the idea. Some will be confused.

But I have a few thoughts / observations.

This must surely be a US Policy and important enough for them, that it found implementation on Indian soil even. This must be something to do with the respect that the Americans want to display towards their own defence personnel.

I walked up to the Indian young man, who was the employee of United Airlines and who was handling the boarding (It was on 6 June by the flight leaving at 11.30 pm), and asked him if Indian army colonels would also have the benefit of this same courtesy? He was visibly shaken up and embarrassed. He said, "No sir, the time has not yet come in our country we can convey our respect as a grateful nation".

I returned back to where my daughter was sitting. She asked me what I had gone for, but I was too embarrassed to tell her the truth, I replied....."Nothing darling, I was checking about the flight". I did not want her to start questioning as to why we, as a nation do not extend the same courtesies as another nation does. I did not want her to start comparing our country with another, to our detriment. I did not want her to raise her eye brows, when on the other hand; I have always been expostulating the glory of our country, to my children and urging them not to succumb to other pressures and to become honest, upright and responsible citizens of India.

Within the US, I took a flight from New York to Miami on 14 June via Delta Airlines. The same story was repeated. But this time I did not go to ask any embarrassing questions. Then I learnt that all US Military personnel are allowed one extra piece of baggage and are all entitled to use the Lounge.

My nourishment was not adversely affected, nor my comfort. My ego was surely a bit deflated. Honestly, I confess, the thought did come to my mind....about whether my spending my entire youth in the Indian Army was worth it?

The men I commanded gave me the respect, my brother officers gave me the camaraderie and bonhomie and warmth. The army life gave me a sense of discipline and personality that has stood by my side all these years. Some of my countrymen still look up to me with warmth and respect when they learn that I am a retired army officer. I feel proud and happy that I am not a Politician or a political stooge.....yes I think it was well worth spending my youth and more (28 years in uniform) with the glorious Indian army.......whether OROP comes through or not!

4. What measures should be adopted for avoiding NPA?

Nonperforming assets are a drain to the banks. The banks in India are adopting various strategies to reduce the non performing assets in their banks and they are also adopting various methodologies by which further addition to NPA portfolio is minimized

In the real sense, in case there is a recovery in principal and instalments due in respect of the loans granted to the banks are received 100%, the question of nonperforming assets do not arise. However, there is no such ideal bank where the NPA is nil. Except banks which were originated recently, all banks are prone to have some portion of their loans and advances as non performing advances

The following are some strategies by which banks are trying to curtail nonperforming assets to a great extent:

Recovery Camps:

Bank personnel jointly approach the defaulting borrowers for repayment at a place and time convenient to both the parties. These are more suited to small loans. Normally the borrowers who had availed small loans will be more in number in rural and semi urban areas rather than urban and metro centres. As such, the banks instead of conducting the recovery camps at their branches, they usually conduct such recovery camps in centres like Panchayat board offices, court buildings, government department buildings etc such recovery camps so that the borrowers find it convenient to attend the recovery camps. Under certain circumstances, the manager in charge of the bank branches along with some branch officials go to each visit each house of the borrowers and recover the instalments due in respect of loans availed by them. This type of recovery camp will be successful in case an advance notice is served on the borrowers mentioning the date of recovery camps

Preference of Claims

Banks should expeditiously and properly claim indemnity from organizations like Deposit Insurance and Credit Guarantee Corporation called DICGC, Export Credit Guarantee Corporation called ECGC, Credit Guarantee Fund Trust for small scale industries, Insurance Companies etc and invoke Government/other personal guarantees to recover loan dues and reduce nonperforming assets.

Compromise Proposals

Compromise routes are adopted by banks, where borrowers experience certain genuine difficulties and where normal recovery is not possible. It involves certain sacrifices on the part of the banks on the principle of "one bird at hand is worth two in the bush". Such proposals can be taken up considering the history of the borrowal account, security available, net worth of the borrower/ guarantor, time value of offer made etc

Technical Write Off

Normally banks decide writing off small loans which have become bad and the recovery is not at all possible in those accounts under any circumstances on account of the facts that the borrower might have been expired; he has no means to repay the loan at any cost and there may be huge losses in respect of the properties etc. This is for the sole purpose of servicing such non performing accounts.

One Time Settlement Scheme

To reduce the absolute amount of nonperforming assets, Government of India along with Reserve Bank of India are announcing one time settlement schemes periodically for the past few years. When the borrowers are alive and when the borrowers are farmers, small entrepreneurs etc and they find it very difficult to pay their dues for various reasons like bad health and fall in their business ventures, , however, they have the inclination to repay their debts to the banks, this type of practice is very much helpful to the borrowers and the lending institutions. Surely the banks are in a position to lose certain portion of their loan amount when they are conducting one time settlement schemes.

Suit Filing:

Filing of suit is taken up as a last resort when all other remedies to recover nonperforming assets fail. Banks can initiate recovery proceedings with or without intervention of the courts of law. To expedite the process, banks should be alert and proactive in all stages of the proceedings. i.e. preparation of plaint, service of summons, written statements, trial of the suit, obtaining decree copy, praying for interim relief, execution of decrees, attachment of the property, arrest of the defendants, if needed etc.

Debt Recovery Tribunals:

The debt recovery tribunal act was passed by Indian Parliament in 1993 with the objective of facilitating the banks and financial institutions for speedy recovery of dues in cases where the loan amount is Rs. 10 lakhs and above. The time limit envisaged under the act is not being adhered to in disposing off the suits because of inadequate infrastructure and shortage of recovery personnel with the DRTs. Nonetheless, the DRT act and subsequent amendment in 2000 have provided a great improvement over the normal legal forum

Lok Adalats:

It is a legal forum for expeditious settlement of loan dues on consensus arrived between the bank and the borrowers mediated by the Lok Adalat

Securitisation Act:

The securitisation and financial assets and enforcement of security interest – SARFAESI act 2002 aims to empower banks as secured creditors to take possession, manage and sell the securities without the intervention of court/tribunal. It also aims at Asset Reconstruction by securitization or Reconstruction Company. However, loan with balance below Rs. 1 lakh unsecured loans and loans against collateral of agricultural land are exempted from the purview of this act.

5. SBI Merger: Pros and cons?

India's largest lender State Bank of India (SBI) formally started merger of 5 associative banks and Bhartiya Mahila Bank with itself.. The merged entity will have India's one-fourth of the deposit and loan market.

Post consolidation, SBI's market share will increase from 17 per cent 22.5-23 percent, while the total business of the merged entity will be over 35 lakh crore rupees.

Against this backdrop, it is pertinent to analyse pros and cons of consolidation in the Indian banking sector.

Arguments in favour consolidation

- India is the fastest growing major economy in the world. To sustain this growth, there is a need for mega banks that only will ensure investments into the large scale infrastructure projects.
- At present, there are a total of 27 public sector banks (PSUs) in the country. Apart from the SBIs, all the remaining banks are regional banks. Hence, consolidation helps in leveraging the benefits of economies of scale.
- Banking sector is suffering from non performing assets (NPAs) problem. To overcome this, the government is resorting to capital infusion. Consolidation will increase capital efficiency, apart from improving the ability of banks to recover bad loans.
- Consolidation will help in leveraging the synergies among the banks that have diverse portfolios, focus areas and coverage areas.
- As the government is the only common owner of all yhr PSUs, the PSBs, the process of consolidation is much easier and effortless.

- Indian companies are going global. Now we are home to many multinational companies that have presence in various sectors of the economy. Again this context, big-ticket Indian banks are the most proper platforms to deliver financial services to them.
- At present, there is not a single Indian bank in the top 50 global banks list. The consolidation is expected to fill tis gap, and consequently, help build the 'Brand India' among international investors.
- International experience is also favourable towards consolidation. Banks in Japan gained a lot as a result of large scale merger and acquisition process between 1990- 2004.

Arguments against consolidation

- Experts argue that consolidation should take place in a positive environment. The present process of consolidation is not driven by the inherent strength of the banking system. It is resorted to escape from the problem of NPAs.
- There are apprehensions among the labour unions that the consolidation will lead to job losses.

6. What do you think about reservations in education and jobs?

We live in a free country and this freedom is a gift of democracy to us. Our constitution gives us the right to freedom and most importantly to exercise this freedom in an equitable manner. At the same time it is incumbent on the part of the state to ensure that equality prevails in all sections of the society.

However in today's time one of the major roadblocks to this equality is the Reservation System.

India being a developing nation is currently facing many challenges and the reservation system being one of them. The biggest question that lies in front of us is whether implementing this reservation system has really helped the downtrodden? A current scenario clearly depicts that the 'lower' castes are still discriminated in their daily lives. To uproot casteism it is important that we fight the reservation system which alone will lead us to development, competency, equality and unity.

The reservation system finds its origin in the age-old caste system of India. The caste system at its birth was meant to divide people on the basis of their occupation like teaching and preaching

(Brahmins), kingship and war (Kshatriya) and lastly business (vaish) etc. but soon it became an instrument to divide the society on caste-basis, creating various walls between different sections of the society. Today we stand divided widely into Hindu, Muslim, SC, ST & OBCs with newer reservations coming up for other different sections of the society like Christians, Kashmiris, Jats, Kashmiri Pandits, Tribals etc.

Firstly we need to understand that the reservation system only divides the society leading to discrimination and conflicts between different sections. It is oppressive and does not find its basis in casteism. It is actually the antithesis of a communal living.

Currently, as per the government policy, 15% of the government jobs and 15% of the students admitted to universities must be from Scheduled castes and for the Scheduled tribes there is a reservation of about 7.5 %. Other than this, the state governments also follow their own reservation policies respectively based upon the population constitution of each state. So nearly 50% seats are reserved.

The Mandal commission was established in 1979 by the central government to identify the socially or educationally backward people. It was also set up to consider the question of seat reservations and quotas for people to redressÂ caste discrimination. It used social, economic, and educational indicators to determine backwardness. But today are these reservations actually being utilized on the above mentioned factors? The answer is prima facie 'NO' because the benefits are being stolen away by the creamy layer.

The Â 93rd Constitutional Amendment allows the government to make special provisions for "advancement of any socially and educationally backward classes of citizens", including their admission in aided or unaided private educational institutions. Gradually this reservation policy is to be implemented in private institutions and companies as well. This move led to opposition from non-reserved category students, as the proposal reduced seats for the General category from the existing 77.5% to less than 50.5% since members of OBCs are also allowed to contest in the General category.

Article 15(4) of our constitution empowers the government to make special provisions for advancement of backward classes. Similarly Article 16 provides for equality of opportunity in matters of employment or appointment to any post under the State.

"Clause 2 of article 16 lays down that no citizen on grounds of religion, race, caste, sex, descent, place of birth, residence or any of them be discriminated in respect of any employment or office under the State."

However clause 4 of the same article provides for an exception by conferring a certain kind of power on the government:

"It empowers the state to make special provision for the reservation of appointments of posts in favour of any backward class of citizens which in the opinion of the state are not adequately represented in the services"

Thus two conditions have to be satisfied:

- The class of citizens is backward
- The said class is not adequately represented.

What is surprising is that our constitution clearly is a reservation-friendly constitution but nowhere in the constitution is the term 'backward classes defined. What actually constitutes a backward class? What are the determinants of a backward class? These questions remain unanswered and it is only with the help of judicial pronouncements that they have been given some meaning. Question arises how can reservations be made for something that has not been defined?

Today when a student applies for an admission in any university, the admissions forms are filled with questions like 'Are you SC/ST or OBC or General Category?' How does it matter which category does he belong to, what matters is his merit. A category cannot decide whether he is eligible for admission or not. There many economically worse off children belonging to the forward classes but they cannot get the fruits of such reservation merely by virtue of belonging to the 'general' category. Sometimes these children belonging to the backward classes do not even deserve and still possess the necessary merit as against a child who studied very hard for months to get a seat, thereby snatching away that seat just because he comes from a particular religion or caste for which our government provides reservation.

Reservation should be purely made on the basis of the economical conditions of the applicant and nothing else. The kind of reservation policy that our government currently follows does nothing but divide the society into different sections.

When the then HRD minister Mr. Arjun Singh introduced 27.5% reservation for OBC in centrally funded educational institutes including IIMs and IITs a petition was moved to the President and the Prime Minister stating that such a reservation will take India back from where she is today. Further "everyone understands the need for all sections of the Indian Society to get an opportunity to be a part of this economy but reservation based on caste is not an answer to this. These policies have been in India since the last 50 years and they have failed to meet their objectives. The government should go into the reasons of the failure. Many students don't make it to the institutes because of the economic reasons and those who do not fall in the reservation criteria don not get a fair opportunity too".

To remove this evil it suggested the following:

- Make education mandatory and free for all till age of 15
- Propose reservation based on economic status
- Provide opportunity to students to earn while they study.

Instead of introducing reservations for these backward classes what is required is to bring about revolutionary changes in our education system at the grass-root level. When proper education is not provided to children belonging to such categories during the primary stage itself then on what basis are the reservations provided at a subsequent stage.

Reservations are nothing but means to prosper the vote banks of politicians. They are hindering the country's growth, development and competency in all aspects. On one hand the preamble of our constitution states that we are a free, democratic and sovereign nation and on the other hand reservation system is chaining all these aspects into its clutches. It is creating disparity and differences amongst the people. The constitution lays down that every child has a right to education and no where expresses that any child belonging to a backward class has a little more of this right than the general category. By reserving one category against another creates a feeling of division which is now resulting in a chaos with every small section of the society asking for it.

Reservations on the basis of caste and not on the basis of condition are bad and unacceptable. Fair and just reservations to uplift the people with poor conditions of life, those who don't have meals to eat, clothes to wear and no home to live in. They shall be made on the basis of factors such as gender as women are more disadvantaged than men since primitive times, domicile, family education, family employment, family property, family income and if any disabilities and traumas. The process of reservation should be such that it filters the truly economically deprived individuals and bring them all to justice.

Thus reservations are anti-thesis of development and equality. We don't need reservations based on castes or religion but only to actually provide aid to those who have minimal resources; and merit should be given equaland due importance in admission procedures as well employment opportunities. This way we would be successful in removing caste discrimination and unite the economically rich together in helping the economically poor, irrespective of their castes.

7. How is Swaach Bharat Abhiyan currently important for India?

India that is Bharat is an ancient civilization. It is considered to be a pious nation, its people are very religious. India is consists of people of various faiths; Hindus, Muslims, Christians, Shikhs, Parsis, Jains etc, and they follow their faiths very devotedly. But it is a sad reality of our country that all the cleanliness and piousness is only confined to religious activities or kitchen. We Indians are not concerned about the filth all around us everywhere; anywhere one looks large mounds of dirt will be found.

It's not in our behaviour to keep our surrounding clean and sanitized. At the most we keep our own houses clean and it is of no concern of ours to be careful about streets, lanes, parks or other public places. Even after 65 years of Independence, it is really shameful that Indians are famous for their unhygienic behaviour.

Recently, a new Government came into power and one of its main priorities are to make India clean. And for the same objective, the Government has launched a scheme in the name of "Swachh Bharat Abhiyan". The Government has associated the Abhiyan with Father of the Nation, Mahatma Gandhi as he was a great champion of the cleanliness cause in the country and throughout his life was involved in activities related to sanitation and hygiene.

What is Swachh Bharat Abhiyan

Swachh Bharat Campaign: The Abhiyan was launched by Prime Minister Narendra Modi on 2nd of October, 2014 at Rajghat, New

Delhi with an aim to make India clean. Aim is to provide sanitation facilities to every family, including toilets, solid and liquid waste disposal systems, village cleanliness, and safe and adequate drinking water supply by 2nd October, 2019. It will be a befitting tribute to the Father of the Nation on his 150th birth anniversary. It is significant that the PM himself is taking very proactive role in making the campaign a success; at Rajghat he started the campaign by cleaning the street himself.

However, it has been clearly declared that the campaign is not only the duty of the Government but each and every citizen of the country is equally responsible to keep the nation clean or swachh.

History of Swachh Bharat Abhiyan

The campaign of clean India movement is the biggest step taken ever as a cleanliness drive till date. On the day of launch of campaign around 3 million government employees including students from schools and colleges had participated in the event to make it popularize globally and make common public aware of it. This event was organized at Rashtrapati Bhavan on 2nd of October in 2014 in the presence of 1500 people. This event was flagged off by the Indian President, Pranab Mukherjee.

Prime Minister, Narendra Modi, had nominated the name of nine famous personalities from business industries, sports and Bollywood to drive the clean India campaign. He also had requested from all nine personalities to invite another nine personalities individually and requested to continue the chain nine people to take this campaign to every Indian living in any corner all around the country.

Narendra Modi has said that this campaign should be taken as the big challenge and must pass the request to invite other nine people individually (just like branching of tree) so that this vision of cleanliness may be completed till 2019 and may India become a clean country forever in the history.

By getting inspired from this Indian campaign, the Indo Nepal Doctors Association has launched a campaign called "Swachh Bharat Nepal – Swasth Bharat Nepal Abhiyan" on 3rd of January in 2015. It was started from the Indo-Nepal Border Region, Sunauli – Belihiya (near birth place of Lord Buddha, holy city of Lumbini, Nepal).

Other programme of the cleanliness in India such as Central Rural Sanitation Programme (CRSP) was started in 1986 all over the country which had focused to construct the individual sanitary latrines for the personal use of the people living below the poverty line. It had focused to convert the dry latrines to the low cost sanitary latrines, to construct latrines especially for rural women with other facilities of hand pump, bathing room, sanitation, washing hands, etc. It was targeted that all the provided facilities should be properly maintained by the village Panchayats. Proper sanitation of the village such as drain systems, soakage pits, disposal of solid and liquid wastes, awareness of health education, awareness for social, personal, household and environmental sanitation etc.

Total Sanitation Campaign (TSC) of cleanliness in India was started in 1999 by the Government of India in order to restructure the Rural Sanitation Programme. Nirmal Gram Puraskar was started in the month of June in 2003 as a sanitation programme to boost the Total Sanitation Campaign. It was a an incentive scheme launched by the Government of India in 2003 to award people for total sanitation coverage, maintaining clean environment as well as making villages open defecation-free villages by the Panchayats, Blocks and Districts.

Nirmal Bharat Abhiyan (NBA) was started in 2012 and then Swachh Bharat Abhiyan in 2014 on 2nd of October. However, all the sanitation and cleanliness programmes run by the Indian government earlier were not as effective as the current Swachh Bharat Abhiyan of 2014.

Gandhi Ji's and His Role on Sanitation:

Mahatma Gandhi was a great champion of cleanliness. He was very much concerned about the dirty roads, streets, temples and specially, harizanbastis of the country. Just after returning from South Africa he noticed very bad state of affairs in India regarding sanitation and cleanliness. He took upon himself to motivate and personally commit towards making the country filth free.

As early as 4th February 1916, while addressing a gathering at the inauguration function of Banaras Hindu University, Gandhi ji spoke about the importance of cleanliness and expressed his pain and anguish about the dirt and filth all around. He gave example of his visit to Vishwanath Temple and spoke about the dirty state of affairs in and around the temple. He said: "Is not this great temple a reflection of our own character?" Sharing his pain he questioned whether the temple would be dirt and filth free after the British had left the country. Thus for him cleanliness was equally important as the freedom of the nation.

Gandhi ji was always of the view that everyone should first be the change he/she wishes to see in the world. Thus, whenever and wherever Gandhi ji would get the opportunity he himself would start cleaning the places. Also, as part of constructive programmes and visits all over the country, apart from preparing people for mass struggle against the British, he also lectured them about the importance of cleanliness and proper sanitation.

In D.G. Tendulkar's "Mahatma", Volume Three, there is a reference to Gandhi leaving Patna in 1934, as part of his Harijan tour, for Orissa. At Champapurhat, he found that there was a dispensary on the grounds of the Gandhi Seva Ashram, and used that occasion to give a lecture on the need to rely not on medicines for a cure, but to prevent disease.

Gandhi ji always emphasise the need to educate villagers on good hygiene and sanitation. According to him, the true function of the Ashram was to educate people how they could avoid disease. Gandhi ji and his volunteers would conduct a mass contact programme with the villagers; they would talk about the necessity of sanitation, about keeping their places clean, and about personal hygiene.

When the villagers near Gandhi's ashram refused to cover excreta with earth believing it to be a bhangi's work and sinful, Gandhi personally supervised the scavenging work in villages. To set an example, he, himself used to go to the villages with a bucket and a broom and would clean the places.

All scavenging work in Gandhi ji's ashram was done by its inmates. No dirt or filth could be found anywhere on the ashram ground. There were pits in which all rubbish was buried. In a separate manure pit, peelings of vegetables and left-over food were dumped. Waste water was used for gardening purposes.

Gandhi ji regularly wrote about the importance of hygiene in his newspaper Harijan. Thus, the Father of our Nation fought not only against the bondages of the British rule but also against the bad practices our people regarding sanitation and hygiene. All his life he inspired and motivated people to maintain personal as well as public hygiene.

Therefore, it is a great gesture and an apt tribute to the Mahatma that the Government has launched the "Swachh Bharat Campaign" on his birth day i. e. on 2nd of October.

Objectives of Swachh Bharat Abhiyan

The campaign of Swachh Bharat launched by the government of India is aimed to accomplish various goals and fulfil the vision and mission of "Clean India" by 2nd of October 2019 which is 150th birth anniversary of the great Mahatma Gandhi. It has been expected that the investment to cost would be over 62000 crore of Indian rupee (means US$ of 9.7 billion). It has been declared by the government that this campaign is taken as "beyond politics" and "inspired by patriotism".

Following are the some important objectives of the Swachh Bharat Abhiyan:

- To eradicate the system of open defecation in India
- To convert the insanitary toilets into pour flush toilets
- To remove the system of manual scavenging
- To make people aware of healthy sanitation practices by bringing behavioural changes in people
- To link people with the programmes of sanitation and public health in order to generate public awareness
- To build up the urban local bodies strong in order to design, execute and operate all systems related to cleanliness.
- To completely start the scientific processing, disposals reuse and recycling the Municipal Solid Waste
- To provide required environment for the private sectors to get participated in the Capital Expenditure for all the operations and maintenance costs related to the clean campaign.

How to Get Involved in the Swachh Bharat Abhiyan

Swachh Bharat Abhiyan is started to make India a clean India by the effort of all the citizens living in the country. It has been clearly declared by the Prime Minister, Narendra Modi that anyone may actively participate in the event anytime. He just need to take snaps of the dirty places and also take snaps of the same places after cleaning them and upload both, before and after snaps on the social media websites like Facebook, Twitter, etc to familiarize and motivate other common people to do the same in order to fulfill the vision of clean India.

After such request by the Indian prime minister to the Indian public, it was started rapidly by the people of India. From the day of launching of event, people became very active and motivated and started doing the same by taking both before and after snaps and uploaded it to the social media websites to make globalize. It was also said by the Narendra Modi that the one who do this would really be appreciated for his/her involvement in the campaign by the government on the social media websites. Many famous personalities of the Bollywood, Tollywood, politicians, sports, business industries, etc such as Aamir Khan, Amitabh Bachchan, Rhithik Roshan, Sachin Tendulkar, Mridula Sinha ji, Anil Ambani, Ramdev Baba, Shashi Tharoor, Kamal Haasan, Priyabka Chopra, M. Venkaiah Naidu, Amit Shah, Salman Khan, team of Tarak Mehta Ka OoltaChashma and many other participated in the campaign according to their own decided dates and uploaded their pictures on the internet on Facebook and Twitter.

It is also done by the students from schools, colleges, universities, and other educational institutions. Youths of the country involving in the daily routine job and other business activities also participated in the event and do the same. All the activities done by famous personalities, students and youths of the country has supported and encouraged common public to do get involved in the campaign very actively. We as an Indian citizen just need to pick up the broom in our hand and clean all the dirty places in our surroundings to make them clean and neat.

Students from most of the schools and colleges had participated in the event in group then why we are back, we also should actively participate in the event. Most of the independent application programme developers have made many mobile applications using mobile technologies to make this campaign a successful campaign. Medias are also boosting this campaign through their articles and news publications. Times of India has also motivated the people towards this campaign by publishing the article under title "Desi companies beat Facebook in 'Swachh' apps race". Another published article is under title "This Indian App Could Change How People Talk to Their Government".

A Nationwide Real Time Monitoring system has also been launched by the Government of India in order construct toilets under this campaign aiming to attain 100% Open Defecation Free India by 2019. A short film on the Swachh Bharat has been made by the NIT Rourkela PHD students to convey most important message of Swachh Bharat to people. We should participate in this mission by meeting our hands together and taking this clean Abhiyan as an important part of our life as the vision of clean India can be achieved through the effort of each and every Indian citizen and not by the effort of government only.

A Movie supporting this Campaign

A movie named as "Toilet: Ek Prem Katha" is released on 11 August 2017. This film is directed by Shree Narayan Singh and co-produced by Akshay Kumar and Neeraj Pandey. Lead roles are played by Akshay Kumar and Bhumi Pednekar. This movie supports the campaign of Swachh Bharat Abhiyan run by the Modi government in order to improve the sanitation conditions and promote the eradication of open defecation especially in the rural areas.

Another Cleanliness Initiative in UP under Swachh Bharat Abhiyan Campaign

The Chief Minister of Uttar Pradesh, Yogi Adityanath, in March 2017 has banned chewing paan, paan masala, ghutka and other tobacco products during duty hours in all the government offices all over the state when he saw betel-juice stained walls, corners during his first visit to the secretariat annexe building. This initiative was started by him to ensure cleanliness in the official buildings.

Celebrities involved in Swachh Bharat Abhiyan

Anil Ambani, Chairman of Reliance Group
Aamir Khan, Actor
Amitabh Bachchan, Actor
Baba Ramdev, Spiritual leader
Chanda Kochhar, Managing director of ICICI Bank
Hrithik Roshan, Actor
Kamal Hassan, Actor
Kapil Sharma, Stand-up Comedian
Manisha Koirala, Actress
Mridula Sinha, Writer in Hindi Literature and Politician

Priyanka Chopra, Actress
Ruby Yadav
Sachin Tendulkar, Former Indian cricketer
Saina Nehwal, Indian Badminton Player
Salman Khan, Actor
Shashi Tharoor, Politician
Team of Taarak Mehta Ka OoltahChashmah, TV Serial

Others celebrities involved in Swachh Bharat Abhiyan are Anupam Kher, Parineeti Chopra, Akshay Kumar, Alia Bhatt, Neha Dhupia, Ajay Devgan, Subash Ghai (filmmaker), Gagan Narang (Indian shooter), Vijender Singh (Indian boxer), Manoj Tiwari, Mary Kom, Nagarjuna, Tamannaah Bhatia, Hema Malini, etc.

8. NSG is the need of the hour for India.

There is a lot of anticipation about the Nuclear Suppliers Group plenary session that is taking place in Seoul on Thursday and Friday. But what exactly is the NSG and why is it crucial for India to be a member of this group? Prime Minister Narendra Modi has convinced several members, including US, Mexico and Switzerland, to allow India on board but with China yet to accept India's inclusion and Pakistan's outright protest against it, the plenary session of 23 and 24 June takes on significant meaning.

Here's a primer:

1. The Nuclear Suppliers Group (NSG) states on its website that it is "a group of nuclear supplier countries that seeks to contribute to the non-proliferation of nuclear weapons through the implementation of two sets of guidelines for nuclear exports and nuclear-related exports." The guidelines includes a principle that states that transfer of nuclear technology will be authorised only on the condition that such a deal will not lead to the proliferation of nuclear weapons. That's why all the member states of the NSG are signatories of the Treaty on the Non-Proliferation of Nuclear Weapons (NPT). The NSG guidelines also complement several other international treaties related to nuclear non-proliferation.
   Prime Minister Narendra Modi speaks with Mexican President Enrique Pena Nieto. Mexico is supporting India's bid for NSG membership. Reuters

2. India is not a member of the NPT. It is a point that China has consistently raised while trying to block India's membership to the NSG. However, China is supporting Pakistan's membership. Pakistan too has not signed the NPT.
3. NSG was set up in response to India's own clandestine nuclear test in 1974, which made New Delhi something of a pariah in the West. Joining the club requires the unanimous approval of all 48 members.
4. Analysts say joining the NSG is chiefly a matter of pride and desire to be taken seriously by some of the world's most powerful nations. Since prompting international technology sanctions and limits on exports by conducting nuclear tests in 1998, India has been eager to gain legitimacy as a nuclear power.
5. Joining the NSG will give India better access to low-cost, clean nuclear energy — important for its economic growth. Nuclear power is one way India, the third-biggest emitter of greenhouse gases, could cut its emissions and reduce air pollution from coal-fired power plants.
6. As Jaideep Prabhu points out in this first post article, NSG membership would put India on a firmer footing to propose the idea of plutonium trade for its thorium programme that has been waiting in the wings. An early adoption of thorium technology would give India enormous energy independence and security.
7. PM Modi is so keen on the NSG membership that he set up a meet with China's President Xi Jinping on the sidelines of the Shanghai Cooperation Organisation (SCO) summit in Uzbekistan's capital Tashkent on Thursday. It is the same day when the NSG plenary session in Seoul begins, a meeting in which India's membership application is expected to come up. Foreign Secretary S Jaishankar is in Seoul to closely monitor the NSG meet.
8. The US has openly supported India's membership to the NSG and even urged other members to do so. "We believe, and this has been US policy for some time, that India is ready for membership and the United States calls on participating governments to support India's application at the plenary session of Nuclear Suppliers Group (NSG)," White House Press Secretary Josh Earnest told reporters. Among others who

have publicly backed India's bid to NSG are Mexico, France, Switzerland, Russia, Japan, UK and Canada.

9. Other than China, countries that are opposing India's inclusion in the NSG are Turkey, South Africa, Ireland and New Zealand.
10. While considering India's membership application, the NSG will also have to consider the fact that accepting this application can pose problems on the processing of applications from Pakistan and Israel, both of whom have not signed the NPT.

9. Rail budget should have merged into general budget much earlier.

After 92 years of seeing them separately, the next year will witness Railway budget merged into Union budget. This move is being lauded for it will be beneficial for the economy at large and there will be positive influence in the development in railways.

During the British reign, having a separate Railway budget made sense because a larger part of the country's GDP depended on railway revenue. The tradition of having the budgets separately continued when India gained freedom even though the revenue from railway continued to go lower than most of the organizations in the public and private sector.

Pros

1. **The scores:** During the British rule Railways took up to 85 percent of the yearly budget while now it has gone down to about 15 percent only. Having separate railway budget stopped making sense long ago but the old tradition was not done away with. Scrapping the old for the renewed and better is always a positive change to look upon.
2. **Better policies:** Now that the Railway budget will be introduced along with the union budget, there will be less wastage of time when a new policy is to be initiated and implemented. Keeping them separate resulted in a lot of drawbacks and hindrances that had to be faced by the railway ministry before it could decide upon a solution.
3. **Party politics:** Minority parties fighting to meet their intentions and ministers of certain states arguing new railways and trains for their region has always been known to result in an everlasting brawl. There will be less of political pressure on

the Railway budget and the centre will have the ultimate hold of the decision making.

4. **Goodbye to annual dividend:** When Rail budget had to be introduced separately, the railways needed to pay an annual dividend to render its budgetary support to the government. The railways will be free of this now and the same fund could now be used in better ways for development the conditions of Indian railways.
5. **The huge loss:** Our railways are running on loss. There are lesser funds for development plans and most of them are wasted in wrongful manner when there emerges a demand from the regional MLA who promised new trains and stoppages for their location during the time of election. When it goes into the hands of finance ministry, it would mean and absolute end to this and a more commercialized distribution of resources.

Cons

1. **The rise and fall:** Henceforth, the distribution and allocation of funds to various departments will all go under the finance ministry, which will take decisions according to rise and fall of budget. A fall in the annual budget will mean a similar cut in the railway and other budgets. This will be something unusual for the railways and they might not react supportively to that.
2. **Conditions of government departments:** The depleting conditions of the various departments under the government have always been prominent. There is lesser attention paid to the responsibilities and everyone is busy sorting out their own means. Railways might see drastic disadvantage if the merging doesn't reap the desired result.
3. **Goodbye to privatization:** There have previously been talks of privatization of Indian railways in order to improve and develop them with world class facilities and cleanliness. It was not well received earlier and after the merging, there will a complete end to any future chances of privatization. At the efficient hands of government employees, nothing big could be expected.
4. **Loss for the railways:** We know how much our parties love making promises and then reducing price to earn the favor of

the voters. Not in their wildest dreams would they want to hike the railway prices and lose the vote bank that flows from commuters. Lesser hikes in price might pose loss for the railways department.

There have been mismanagement of the highest order in Indian railways and if there are chances of seeing it improve, merging it with the Union budget is just the solution that could help. The falling revenue and more projects for new trains and stoppages have been a difficult project for the railway ministry which took the right step by merging the two budgets.

Discussion

- **RE: Merging Railway budget into Union budget - Pros and Cons -Madhuri (08/07/17)**

Giving cons in such a way is very anti governmental which can not be encouraged. Now a days we can't at least its tough to see anti corruption country and ruling. So, we should at least be happy that we r being some what beneficial because of government. Coming to cons many other can be given like as state government role there might be hindrances in regional railway developments and new lines to backward areas and if we include current issues there was no compensation given to railways on running trains in non- profitable lines (happy thing is now PMO has ordered to give the compensation). Every new initiative has cons the only thing is with better implementation and way forwards we can overcome them..

- **RE: Merging Railway budget into Union budget - Pros and Cons -kruti (09/23/16)**

I agree with the pros. however, if the cons are written for competitive exams like UPSC mains then I am afraid it is not at all according to the standard. For competitive exams answers, we can not blame officials or directly claim that the officials are corrupted and the politicians are invariably cheaters. I am sure there is a better way to present the cons. we have to be very diplomatic while writing answers. thank you.

10. Women employment is possible through mass awareness rather than launching programmes.

In promoting women's empowerment it was critical that the international community systematically link women to the development agenda, speakers told the Third Committee (Social,

Humanitarian and Cultural) today, as it continued its discussion on the advancement of women.

As nearly four dozen speakers took the floor to urge further international cooperation in advancing gender equality and to outline specific steps being taken by their national Governments on that front, economic empowerment was frequently highlighted as the surest route to improving women's social status.

To this end, several delegations emphasized the feminine face of poverty and suggested that efforts to advance women and initiatives to promote sustainable economic growth were mutually reinforcing. Thus, strategies for one area should also account for the other.

Thailand's representative said that, in her country, as in many others, women were the primary contributors to the country's economic growth. The Thai Government was working to reverse the feminization of poverty, embarking on strategies to improve women's education, health and empowerment. Overall, its efforts aimed to both protect the rights of, and promote opportunities for, women throughout the economic and social development process.

Echoing this focus on development's gender dimension, a number of African countries underlined the growing awareness of the crucial role of women in development and the need for their participation in decision-making processes to ensure sustainable development.

The representative of the United Republic of Tanzania said that, to enable women's economic empowerment, her Government actively promoted savings and credit societies in both rural and urban areas. Women also benefited from the Tanzania Social Action Fund, while a Government-established women's bank provided training and credit that complemented other microfinancing and entrepreneurship programmes.

She stressed that her country, like other countries both on the African continent and elsewhere, was particularly concerned with addressing the economic situation of rural women. Much of its focus was on ensuring women's access to, and ownership of, land since the majority of rural women depended on agriculture for their livelihood. She said it was imperative to "reverse the neglect" in official development assistance and Government spending on rural women.

Indonesia's representative sounded a note of caution in the discussion on economic empowerment by highlighting an emerging danger that seemed to be the result of women's advancement in this area. She said that as women gained more opportunities in the labour market, there was a simultaneous increase of informal work and migration among them. That trend was not necessarily negative, but a high degree of insecurity had been associated with migrant workers in the informal sector. This was particularly true for women, who were more susceptible to acts of violence.

Several other speakers underscored the dangers facing women migrant workers. The representative of the Philippines noted these women, who often worked at the lowest ends of the labour spectrum, were among the first to be laid off, as a result of the economic and financial crisis. Further, violence was also being reported in free trade and export-processing zones, where many young women migrants were hired on temporary or insecure contracts. In light of such information, her delegation planned to table a draft resolution on violence against women migrant workers, bringing attention to this phenomenon and calling for attention to the problems this subset of women faced.

Sri Lanka's representative expressed strong support for efforts by United Nations agencies to promote targeted measures to protect women migrant workers. Those notable measures included strengthening contractual agreements, control over recruitment agencies and information campaigns, in addition to general efforts to encourage Member States to implement relevant legislation. For its part, his Government had negotiated with several countries to which migrant women were sent to ensure their welfare and protection.

Throughout the day, many delegations also highlighted the increased participation of women in both the public and private sector. Others pointed to ongoing legislative and judicial reforms that were expanding social protections to women and eliminating traditional barriers to their advancement.

The representatives of Kazakhstan, Iran, Nicaragua, Bolivia, Republic of Korea, Liechtenstein, Russian Federation, Colombia, Monaco, Venezuela, Senegal, Syria, Côte d'Ivoire, Kyrgyzstan, Nigeria, Jordan, Australia (also on behalf of Canada and New Zealand), Sri Lanka, Namibia, El Salvador, Slovenia, Democratic People's Republic of Korea, Swaziland, India, Kenya, Israel,

Singapore, Poland, San Marino, Yemen, Ukraine, Bangladesh, Mongolia, Afghanistan, Argentina, Bahrain, Libya, Maldives, Dominican Republic and Djibouti also spoke during the general discussion on the advancement of women. A youth delegate from the Republic of Korea also spoke.

Delegates from Japan, United States, Democratic People's Republic of Korea and Cuba spoke in exercise of the right reply.

Also today, the Committee heard the introduction of draft resolutions on youth, cooperatives, social development, family, ageing and the African Institute on the Prevention of Crime. The representatives of Portugal, Mongolia, Sudan and Uganda introduced the drafts.

The Committee will meet again at 10 a.m., Wednesday, 14 October, to conclude its discussion on the advancement of women and to take up issues relating to the rights of children.

Background

The Third Committee met this morning to continue its general discussion on the advancement of women. (For more details see Press Release GA/SHC/3949 of 12 October.)

It was also expected to hear introductions of six draft resolutions under the agenda item on social development and one draft resolution under the agenda item on crime prevention and criminal justice.

Introduction of Resolutions

The representative of Portugal introduced the resolution on policies and programmes involving youth (document A/C.3/64/L.4), explaining that the text was based on several previous related resolutions (Assembly resolution 62/126 of 2007 and the Commission on the Status of Women resolution 47/1 of 2009), and on information contained in the Secretary-General's report on progress and constraints faced in ensuring the well-being of youth and encouraging their participation in society. The report addressed 11 of 15 priority areas in the Programme of Action for youth, including, among others, situations of armed conflict, girls and young women, HIV/AIDS, information and communications technology, intergenerational issues, delinquency, and leisure activities. The other 4 areas — education, employment, globalization, and hunger and poverty — were addressed in a report published in 2007.

She said the proposed resolution would emphasize that all 15 areas were interrelated, and would call on States to consider the goals and targets of the Secretary-General in his report at the national level, so as to facilitate the monitoring of progress towards the goals set out in the Action Plan. It would request the Secretary-General to develop indicators related to the World Programme on Youth to assist States to assess the situation of youth. As in the past, the text would acknowledge the contribution of youth, and have Member States consider including youth representatives in their delegations. The youth added value to debates by suggesting new wording and bringing an enthusiasm that invigorated discussions. Member States were currently in the process of merging their different proposals. The text was not a procedural resolution, but a complex one. But, she harboured a firm belief that States could overcome any difficulties and arrive at a consensus text.

Next, the representative of Mongolia introduced the resolution on cooperatives in social development (document A/C.3/64/L.10). She said cooperatives as business enterprises offered a model that was particularly relevant in difficult economic times and instances of market failure.They supported entrepreneurs, raised participants' incomes and helped to enhance social inclusion and community building, among other things. The current food, financial and fuel crises, along with climate change, posed tremendous challenges to the income and food security of millions of people. Taking into account the Secretary-General's recommendations, her country was planning to propose 2012 as the International Year of Cooperatives to encourage Governments to establish policies conducive to the growth of cooperatives, raise awareness of cooperatives and their contribution to development, and to encourage people to organize cooperatives to address their economic needs. The Year was not envisioned as a year of celebration, but a year of productive work towards the promotion of cooperatives. Passage of the draft resolution would not lead to budgetary financial implications.

In light of the ongoing crises, she said agriculture and financial cooperatives deserved attention. They contributed to long-term solutions and more resilient and inclusive financial systems, helping farmers improve their earnings and lowering credit costs, and promoting better marketing and distribution of products. They improved farm productivity. Access to credit was one of the challenges to farming, and cooperatives were more involved in financing, both directly and indirectly. The text invited Governments and others to promote the growth of cooperatives through: affordable financing; the provision of new farming techniques; investment in infrastructure, such as irrigation; strengthening marketing mechanisms; and promoting women in agricultural activities. The current financial crisis had led to greater appreciation of the role of international financial institutions, such as financial cooperatives, which contributed to poverty reduction by providing savings products and access to credit to small enterprises and small depositors. The text would invite Governments and international organizations to promote the growth of financial cooperatives to meet the goal of inclusive finance. She expressed hope that the resolution would receive unanimous support.

The representative of Sudan introduced the draft resolution on implementation of the outcome of the World Summit for Social Development and of the twenty-fourth special session of the General Assembly (document A/C.3/64/L.9). He said the draft aims to highlight all three pillars of the Copenhagen summit, namely, poverty eradication, achievement of full and productive employment, and social integration. It further emphasized that all three were mutually reinforcing and should be pursued to guarantee social development. It takes into account the February 2009 discussion in the Commission on Social Development, which took social integration as its theme. Accordingly, it also includes language from the Secretary-General's report on social integration (document A/64/157). It further takes into account the world financial and economic crisis and its impact on social development, and invites the Secretary-General to submit to the General Assembly at its sixty-fifth session a report on the world crises and its impact on social development. Finally, it incorporates the concerns of the "Group of 77" developing countries and China, vis-à-vis social development.

He next introduced a draft resolution on follow-up to the tenth anniversary of the International Year of the Family and beyond (document A/C.3/64/L.7). He said the Group of 77 and China was submitting this draft, as it had in recent years, to urge Member States to continue to integrate a family perspective into national policymaking. The text highlights as a major objective of the International Year of the Family the strengthening of the capacity of national institutions to formulate, implement and monitor national laws that further the needs of the family. Moreover, it seeks to encourage the incorporation of family-oriented policies into national strategies aimed at social integration. Recalling the upcoming twentieth anniversary of the International Year of the Family in 2014, it asks the Secretary-General to recommend to Member States the appropriate ways to mark that anniversary.

He then introduced a resolution on 2010: International Year of the Youth: Dialogue and Mutual Understanding (document A/ C.3/64/L.8), saying it was a new text. The Group of 77 and China had noticed that the current world situation had widened the gap between North and South, with growing manifestations of poverty and marginalization. There seemed to be a growth of hatred and xenophobia and widened misunderstandings between different "systems of human civilization". Youth represented a vulnerable group facing multiple socio-economic challenges, with the potential to play an important role in the development of their countries. To guarantee their active integration into society and international life, including United Nations forums, there was a pressing need to formulate a new approach for encouraging their participation in areas such as health, education, work, culture, entertainment, security, and the family environment.

In addition, he said too many youth were falling into poverty, illiteracy, unemployment and becoming HIV positive. The world needed to renew its commitment to address youth issues. It needed, more than ever, to promote among youth universal values, such as tolerance, moderation, respect of others, rejection of all violence and extremism, and a culture of citizenship, solidarity, peace and dialogue. The text would call on States to proclaim 2010 as the International Youth Year, and to organize under the auspices of the United Nations and its partners a world youth conference. Informal consultations on the draft were ongoing.

He also introduced a resolution on follow-up to the Second World Assembly on Ageing (document A/C.3/64/L.6), tabled annually by the Group of 77, building on previous resolutions on the same theme. It incorporated recommendations of the Secretary-General, as contained in his report on the issue. The text would have nations build the capacity, and promote the inclusion of, the ageing population through specific, ageing mainstreaming efforts. Its provisions would ensure that older persons had access to information on their rights, and would stress a gender perspective in all policy areas of ageing. It would have States eliminate discrimination on the basis of age, and address cases of neglect and abuse of older persons. It would invite States to consider how best to improve international norms and standards pertaining to older persons. It would request the Secretary-General to submit a report at the next session of the Assembly on the current status of the social situation and well-being of older persons, taking into account observations from the conference relating to ageing due to take place early next year. Informal consultations on the text were ongoing.

Turning to the agenda item on crime prevention and criminal justice, Uganda's representative introduced the draft text on the United Nations African Institute for the Prevention of Crime and the Treatment of Offenders (document A/C.3/64/L.14). She said it sought to update General Assembly resolution 63/196 on the Institute, drawing from the Secretary-General's report on it and its work. She noted that the draft text would be undergoing informal consultations to ensure that areas of concern were addressed. This year, more amendments to the preamble paragraphs reflected some of these emerging areas of concern. Moreover, several new preamble paragraphs were added. They included paragraphs 4, 6, 8, and 9. Preamble paragraph 4 was added to address the link between climate change and poverty, as well as the link between poverty and crime. Other preamble paragraphs recognized initiatives undertaken by the Institute to ensure that it serviced needs in the region, despite its crippling lack of resources. The African Group recognized that Africa could not afford to ignore the impact of new and growing crime rates, she said. It, thus, called on the General Assembly to recognize the necessity of continuing to support the Institute as a matter of international crime prevention.

Statements

BYRGANYM AITIMOVA (Kazakhstan) said her Government attached great importance to the recent General Assembly resolution on a more effective United Nations entity focused on gender equality and women's empowerment. Her country had actively engaged in informal consultations on the issue and would welcome the establishment of the composite gender entity. Given adequate institutional capacity, the entity would become a stronger advocate for gender-based rights and women's empowerment, promote effective system-wide gender mainstreaming and be a better fund-raiser for that aspect of human development. Kazakhstan supported a well-balanced organizational structure, avoiding duplication and unclear terms of reference. Having fully endorsed the Secretary-General's UNiTE campaign, Kazakhstan saw the importance of channelling all stakeholders' efforts into practical measures "on site". It made its first contribution to the Trust Fund in Support of Actions to Eliminate Violence against Women and, nationally, had intensified implementation of gender equality laws. It aimed to adopt a domestic violence law in 2009.

She remarked on the international community's intense focus on modern forms of slavery, seen in the trafficking of human beings, and instances of sexual and labour exploitation, particularly towards girls and women. Kazakhstan welcomed the numerous initiatives in that area, and nationally was paying great attention to modernizing its legislation to ensure an adequate response. It was also improving its criminal justice system to close loopholes that would set violators free. Non-governmental stakeholders had an active voice in hosting regular training for potential victims of trafficking and/or sexual exploitation. The economic and financial crisis tended to promote trafficking in human beings, and so improving "social determinants" was considered integral to preventing that disgraceful activity from happening. Kazakhstan was using a dual approach to provide economic security to women, by maintaining its high level of maternity care and childcare, and guaranteeing equal opportunities for both women and men in the area of economic development. It was working to build women's capacity for entrepreneurship, especially those living in rural areas. Indeed, achieving gender equality was no less important than meeting the goals of global safety and sustainable development.

MOHAMMAD POURNAJAF (Iran), recalling the meaning of "gender mainstreaming" as defined by the Economic and Social Council in July 1997, said the Commission on the Status of Women had conducted, in 2005, a review of the commitments made in Beijing and found that women did not yet enjoy human rights on the same basis as men. While 2005 had been a target date for the revocation of discriminatory laws, that date had come and gone with many of them still in force. It was high time to repeal them as a long overdue remedy to women's plight, and a response to the pleas of women's advocates around the world. Action, not words, was needed to mainstream "gender justice", and, in this, mentoring programmes could be extremely helpful in putting the plan of action on the right track. A gender-perspective approach was needed, but finding the right balance remained a challenge. Team-building skills that aimed to foster cooperation in familial relations, rather than antagonism or a hierarchical approach, should be advanced.

He stressed that climate change's link with poverty eradication was another unresolved issue. Adapting to climate change would affect agriculture, food security and water management in rural areas. Since most rural livelihoods were traditionally "women's tasks" in developing countries, policies that affected them had to be considered for their impact on women. This was also true in terms of human trafficking. Preventive activities should include education about the dangers of trafficking, in combination with economic opportunities at home and the establishment of legal migration channels for women. Armed conflicts, natural disaster and other crises had created new vulnerabilities for women. While often full of promise, post-conflict and post-crisis processes often failed to address the prevailing gender, class and ethnic imbalances and tended to deepen existing disparities, or create new ones. Accordingly, all States should recognize that economic and social security was crucial to advancing women's capabilities. The linkages between violence to women and their access to economic and social rights should also be considered. Still, formulating universal law on preventing and combating domestic violence was the most promising legal measure, and the gap between the normative framework and practice should be bridged.

MARIAM MWAFFISI (United Republic of Tanzania), aligning herself with the Group of 77 and China, said her country was committed to the attainment of gender equality and women's empowerment. She thanked Tanzania's bilateral donors, as well as the European Union and various specialized organs of the United Nations for their support to its national gender machineries and gender mainstreaming efforts. Notable examples of achievement included the achievement of gender parity in education enrolment and the formation of science camps for girls. The gender dimension programme at the University of Dar es Salaam had greatly contributed to the increase in women in tertiary institutions taking science subjects. The Government had surpassed the 30 per cent threshold for women in public service and parliament; it was now reaching 50 per cent.

To enable the economic empowerment of women, she said the Government had actively promoted savings and credit societies in both rural and urban areas. Women benefited from the Tanzania Social Action Fund, while a women's bank established by the Government provided training, in addition to credit. The bank complemented microfinancing and entrepreneurship development programmes being provided by grass-roots organizations. But, violence against women continued to be a challenge, leading the Government to establish a national action plan on the prevention and eradication of violence against women and children. In addition, the President had launched a campaign to "say no to violence" against women in Tanzania.

In rural areas, she said the Government had enacted laws to ensure women's access to, and ownership of, land. This was important, given that a majority of rural women depended on agriculture for their livelihood. It was imperative to "reverse the neglect" in official development assistance and government spending on rural women. She was encouraged by the attention paid at the United Nations towards gender equality, and believed that a stronger gender entity with a strong field presence would enhance the cause. She looked forward to forthcoming negotiations on that issue.

MARIA RUBIALES DE CHAMORRO (Nicaragua), endorsing the statements made on behalf of the Group of 77 and China and the Rio Group, said the revolutionary struggle to transform society, as elaborated in the Beijing Declaration and Platform for Action, had provided a framework for her country's domestic legislation and the drawing up of national plans and programmes. At present, a national development plan, a social welfare system, a 12-part gender policy and an institute for women sought to promote a gender perspective in all of Nicaragua's institutions. A 50 per cent quota for women had been established for all Government positions. A gender violence unit had been set up to ensure that justice was sufficiently enacted for women and girls. The national police force was headed by a woman and, through its units for women and children, the force worked to provide preventive and rehabilitative care for victims of sexual violence. The judiciary had also been organized to allow for sexual crimes to be addressed.

Ensuring that women's rights were respected was not just a matter of social policy for Nicaragua, she said. Rather, it extended to development and other policies. Women were active participants in the national literacy campaign. Regarding health, maternal mortality had been significantly reduced through training of expectant mothers, better follow up and early identification of risks. To ensure that rural women received proper care for a safe birth, a system of maternal houses had been set up to provide care 24 hours a day. To prevent sexual discrimination in the workplace, women were being trained to recognize their labour rights. Still, Nicaragua's Government regretted the fact that violence against migrant women continued at the international level. Those who perpetrated this violence should be brought to justice. Nicaragua was also promoting global action to prevent human trafficking.

INGRID SABJA (Bolivia), aligning herself with the Group of 77 and China, said women in Bolivia's rural areas, particularly indigenous women, were still subject to discrimination and sex segregation. She remarked that what women did in their homes could cushion the effects of the economic crisis. It was time to revise the idea that only paid work was productive work; household work should be recognized as real work, as well. Recognizing that fact was the first step in achieving the principle of shared responsibility between women and men.

She said Bolivia's new political constitution recognized that women's rights were part and parcel of universal human rights, and the gender perspective was all-pervasive in that text. The constitution incorporated principles of gender equality as a means of dismantling an old system replete with discrimination, and of allowing women to participate more actively in political life. It provided for their access to education at all levels, extended health care and social security to them, as well as their rights to land. A new quota law in public service required that the lists of candidates put forward by political parties were 50/50 men and women. Around 34 per cent of the seats in the Constituent Assembly were held by women, many of whom were indigenous. The President had indigenous women in his cabinet. In addition, the national plan for equal opportunity sought to bring people of different communities together to promote a life without power imbalances. She added that the new constitution indicated that women had the right to free maternal care of an "inter cultural nature". Women were given a mother-child allowance to reduce maternal and infant mortality, and to boost infant nutrition.

She looked forward to meeting with other States on system-wide coherence, including on defining the new gender architecture. It was essential to ensure "cross-cutting inclusion of gender perspectives" in all agencies at the United Nations.

HONG WOOK-JIN (Republic of Korea) said her Government was particularly focused on women migrants seeking jobs and new lives through international marriages. It had established social mechanisms for securing those women's rights, especially in the face of discrimination or violence, and to support their full integration into Korean society. It had established the "1577-1366 Centre" that provided emergency assistance services and ordinary counselling in eight different languages for women migrants married to Korean men. The centre provided 24-hour service all year round. Turning challenges of a global nature, she expressed concern over violence against women, and voiced support for Security Council resolutions calling for increasing the number of women in senior positions at the United Nations. On climate change, she urged that gender considerations be included in the climate change agreement in December. The success or failure to overcome such gaps depended on the United Nations' capacity to pursue gender equality and women's empowerment and, to that end, her Government looked forward to the early establishment of a composite gender entity.

She then ceded the floor to a youth delegate from the Republic of Korea, who suggested solutions focused on three main topics in the World Programme of Action for Youth: the environment, employment and the empowerment of girls and young women. She said, with environmental degradation threatening the lives of women, international collaboration should be made to recognize gender equality as an integral part of creating an environmentally sustainable society. Also, in light of the global financial crisis — in which women faced higher projected rates of unemployment and higher vulnerability to losing jobs in industries and services where they could practice a decent profession — the international community must find ways to prevent women from turning to unpaid or unstable jobs. The Government of the Republic of Korea currently had a basic plan for equal employment and a work-family life reconciliation programme to help women handle their multiple responsibilities, and had designated 50 support organizations as "new occupation centres for women", which were one-stop shops for employment services.

BARBARA STEFAN (Liechtenstein) said that investing in gender equality meant investing in progress. The empowerment of women was a precondition for development and was also reflected in Millennium Development Goal 3. However, due to ongoing discrimination and inequality, women remained disproportionately affected by poverty, hunger and food insecurity. In that context, she recalled that achieving the Millennium Development Goals and the advancement of women were mutually reinforcing, and immediate action should be taken accordingly. Liechtenstein looked forward to the early establishment of the new composite gender entity, which would help consolidate existing strengths and create synergy to improve the contribution of the United Nations to gender equality.

She welcomed United Nations efforts, campaigns and initiatives aimed at eliminating violence against women and its devastating social, economic and humanitarian consequences. States had an obligation to protect women from all forms of violence, hold perpetrators accountable and provide justice and remedies for the victims. Although the development of national and international legal norms, standards and policies was progressing, they had to be fully implemented around the world. Indeed, Liechtenstein was deeply concerned about the shocking increase of sexual violence in conflicts around the world. Even after conflicts ended, high levels of sexual violence could persist, meaning that women remained excluded from formal decision-making processes in post-conflict environments. It was, therefore, essential to increase the participation of women in conflict resolution and peace processes. To this end, she welcomed the Secretary-General's appointments of more women to senior positions, generally, and field missions particularly.

She also expressed support for Security Council resolutions 1325 (2000) and 1820 (2008) which emphasized the responsibility of all States to put an end to impunity and to prosecute those responsible for war crimes, including acts of gender violence. But, formal justice systems often lacked the required resources to prosecute perpetrators. Thus, she welcomed the call of resolution 1888 (2009) for the Secretary-General to offer expertise to national authorities to strengthen the rule of law. Protection and support to victims should also be provided, particularly to ensure they can testify freely and without fear of retaliation.

EKATERINA LAKHORA (Russian Federation) said the Convention on the Elimination of Discrimination against Women, the outcome documents of the four world conferences on women and the Millennium Development Goals had been the starting points for a reformation of Russian society. The principle of gender equality was gaining traction and, pursuant to federal law, justice was administered in an equal way regardless of gender. Government programmes contained many initiatives that promoted the issues most pressing for women, including comprehensive family support and protection of motherhood and childhood. Even the financial crisis had not changed this priority. Indeed, today, for the first time in Russia's history, demography was regarded as of equal importance as security. This instilled hope and confidence in Russian women.

She said there had been a significant change in the scope of voluntary organizations being involved in elections. As a result, women were gaining increasing numbers of elected positions. In the Duma, they now held 14 per cent of the seats. Women were also heading up a number of important ministries. This often meant that women were better accounted for in public policies. Women were also enjoying progress in the private sector, and the Russian Federation now ranked third in terms of women employed in business. Moreover, gender equality was impossible without the active participation of civil society. Broad scale gender awareness programmes had been held in all parts of Russian society. Many women's organizations also had activities to promote equal rights and to draw the attention of Government authorities to social ills that particularly affected women. In her country, it was recognized that only by cooperating with international organizations and sharing experiences could progress be made.

CLAUDIA BLUM (Colombia), aligning herself with the Rio Group and the Group of 77 and China, said her country's 2006-2010 national development plan was gender sensitive. Various affirmative action programmes benefited women in specific ways to: prevent violence against them; improve employment and development prospects; improve political participation; and provide access to education and culture. Laws covering violence and discrimination against women were strengthened in 2008 by the passage of a new law. At the same time, the Government sought to improve women's access to justice through education and awareness-raising strategies targeted at women, as well as improved training among public officials. Colombia also agreed with the Secretary-General on the importance of including a gender perspective in humanitarian assistance; in disarmament, demobilization and reintegration; and in assisting victims of violence. Its budget for reparation to victims of violence had been strengthened in 2009 by a new budget plan.

On poverty eradication, she described various strategies adopted by her country to promote microcredit among rural women, and to improve child nutrition and education through cash transfers. In addition, the country would tackle gender discrimination at work through the equal employment agenda signed by major business associations earlier in the year. A gender affairs observatory was developing a database, by which the Government would evaluate its gender policies. Turning to the protection of migrant workers, she pointed to two resolutions that her country, with others, had promoted at the Human Rights Council. One related to maternal mortality and morbidity and promoted further action on that issue. The second dealt with the elimination of discrimination against women. International cooperation was important to support national efforts to advance gender equality. To that end, Colombia had great hopes for the new gender architecture at the United Nations, and would support the process of establishing the composite gender entity.

ISABELLE PICCO (Monaco) said the Secretary-General's global campaign was a first step in eliminating violence against women around the world. The Security Council's recent adoption of resolution 1888 (2009), which recognized the link between the maintenance of peace and security and the prevention of the sexual violence that was often used as a war tactic against civilians, should bring an end to the impunity that many perpetrators of that sexual violence enjoyed. Monaco wished to join its voice with those supporting the appointment of a Special Representative to address sexual violence in armed conflict and coordinate all United Nations activities, in that regard. It should be underlined that progress made in implementing the global strategy to aid and support victims of sexual violence committed by United Nations personnel was part of a broader context. The increase in the number of women in peacekeeping missions helped ensure this work. Monaco welcomed the ministerial debate held at the beginning of the General Assembly's sixty-fourth session that was headed by Hillary Clinton.

She went on to welcome the General Assembly's decision to reinforce the institutional mechanisms in ways that favoured gender quality. The education of girls and boys was still the cornerstone of prevention. Monaco was convinced that the Secretary-General was in the position to appoint an Under-Secretary-General to head up the Organization's work to promote gender equality and women's advancement. Monaco's Government had, for several years, undertaken a campaign to combat all forms of violence. It had set up programmes throughout Africa to promote women's empowerment and the equal representation of women.

JORGE VALERO (Venezuela), aligning himself with the Group of 77 and China and the Rio Group, said women were the invisible sex in many parts of the world. They were victims of oppression and stereotypes. His Government had launched a new development model guaranteeing equality between men and women and respect for the human rights of all. The Constitution used neutral, non-sexist terminology. In it, domestic work was recognized as a wealth-creating activity that added value to society. Women took part in decision-making and contributed to the building of the new social order. The Government delivered assistance to women with disabilities, indigenous women and women of African descent through local community organizations.

Gender mainstreaming was part of government policy, he continued. The country's legal framework ensured the protection of all women's rights, and the incorporation of women in society and the "production system". The Ombudsman's unit had established a special unit on women's rights. There was a labour law covering working conditions relevant to women, such as protection for mothers, security for women at work, and health leave. Social service law looked at protecting the family and women with children, as well as the care of older persons. Maternity and paternity policies were in place to promote joint responsibility of raising girls and boys. Other laws were in place to help the unemployed, including women heads of household and victims of gender violence.

He said the country practiced a policy of 50/50 parity on electoral lists, leading more women to stand for political office. It had new institutions with innovative programmes to overcome inequalities, such as the ministry for the empowerment of women and gender equality, the development bank for women, and others. Subsidized loans had led to the emergence of women's cooperatives. "Mothers' missions", a group of grass-roots organizations, provided social coverage to women and promoted inclusivity. There were laws designed to bring about a violence-free environment for women, including the Inter-American Convention on Violence against Women. The Government was also taking preventive action against trafficking in women.

LEYSA SOW (Senegal), endorsing the statement made on behalf of the Group of 77 and China, said there was growing awareness of the crucial role of women in development and the need for their participation in decision-making processes to ensure sustainable development. Women were still underrepresented in economic life. Democracy and good governance were broadly subject to the gender dynamic, which also affected the development progress. It was increasingly clear that the changes in mindset and behaviour that were needed for gender equality would not be achieved by 2015, and more action was needed. Through Millennium Development Goal 3, which addressed gender equality and women's empowerment, the international community had highlighted the need for policies and programmes that had a gender component. A cross-cutting approach should be taken in relation to the issue, especially in African countries, where women typically supported the family and often supported the man, even though he acted as head of the family.

She said this meant, in broad terms, that the gender differences of men and women had resulted in social inequality. Although there were policies that sought to rebalance the relationship, they were often just band-aids. Senegal had, however, made some developments in advancing the situation of women. It had ratified all the relevant instruments. Provisions in the new constitution guaranteed equality. In 1999, Senegal had voted against female genital mutilation. A national action centre for women had been set up to build capacity for women's issues. A women's credit programme provided accessible management mechanisms for women. Girls' school enrolment had increased and a cross-sectoral policy for families had been enacted, as had a family rights monitoring body that included a women's rights unit.

VANASSUDA SUDHIDHANEE (Thailand) declared her country's commitment to its obligations under the Women's Anti-Discrimination Convention, the Beijing Declaration, and the outcome of the twenty-third special session of the General Assembly on women. It looked forward to the review of the Beijing Platform next year. Thailand's candidate to the Convention's monitoring Committee, SaisureeChutikul, was also an adviser to the working group on the establishment of an Association of Southeast Asian Nations (ASEAN) commission on the protection and promotion of the rights of women and children. Thailand's own women's development plan aimed to protect the rights of, and promote opportunities for, women to participate fully in the economic and social development process. As in many other countries, women were the primary contributors to the country's economic growth. But, poverty had a feminine face. The Thai Government was working to reverse the feminization of poverty, embarking on strategies to improve women's education, health and empowerment.

Continuing, she said Thailand had laws in place to strengthen gender equality, including giving women the right to retain their own surnames and titles after marriage. The Government was seeking to address cultural barriers that prevented women from stepping outside prescribed roles. Today, it was more common for Thai women to make career choices across a wide spectrum of jobs, including medical doctors, judges, engineers, peacekeepers and peace builders and so on. Thailand looked forward to negotiations on the new United Nations gender architecture, noting that now was a good time to ask, "Have we achieved the ideal launched 15 years ago?" Gender equality was not only a woman's concern, but must be addressed by society as a whole.

WARIF HALABI (Syria), joining the statement made on behalf of the Group of 77 and China, reasserted her country's commitment to the Beijing Declaration and Platform of Action and the outcome document of the twenty-third special session of the General Assembly, among other documents related to women's advancement. Noting that these documents called for serious and intensified strategies to promote gender equality, she said that Syria worked to implement their provisions by, among other things, consolidating measures already adopted leading to the political, economic and social empowerment of Syrian women.

She said Syria's State planning department had drawn up a national plan for eradicating poverty and eliminating the discrimination against women. This map, which was created by the Department of Agriculture, assessed the needs of women. Syria also sought, each year, to implement the current version of its 5-

year plan. As a result, a reduction in the social gaps between men and women had been seen, as had an increase in women occupying leadership posts. The earmarking of budgetary resources to promote social development and women's interests were the main means of achieving the State's objectives, and the national budget made a priority of social and economic development. Under its tenth 5-year plan, a budget had been drawn up that took the general needs of improving society into account.

The Government had been working to free up the occupied Syrian Golan and to enact a lasting solution that would end women's suffering under Israeli occupation, she said. Yet, it should be noted that these efforts impeded development, since resources were sucked into the effort, as well as into the defence budget. Finally, she emphasized that eliminating violence against women was critical. Yet, all approaches towards that goal should take into account national circumstances.

EMILIENNE BOBI ASSA (Côte d'Ivoire), aligning herself with the Group of 77 and China, said, as the international community cast its eyes on the fifteenth anniversary of the Beijing Declaration, it was important to take stock of the situation facing women today. She thanked the United Nations system for its support in helping her country implement the Beijing Declaration. As a result, significant progress had been made in gender equality and women's empowerment. This was reflected in the country's constitution, which prohibited gender-based discrimination and called for equality between men and women. A Ministry of Family, Women and Social Affairs was established in 2006 to coordinate implementation of the Beijing Declaration. Further, Government ministries had established "gender cells" to strategize the implementation, follow up and assessment of gender policies. The Government was also working towards a model law to codify the principles enshrined in a Presidential Declaration on equality of opportunity, signed in 2007, and a poverty reduction strategy paper with a gender dimension, covering the period from 2009 to 2015, had been adopted in January.

She noted that fighting violence against women was central to the Beijing Declaration, and welcomed the Security Council's adoption of resolutions on women, peace and security with provisions to protect civilians against any form of sexual violence. Those resolutions also contained provisions to punish the perpetrators. To encourage women's participation in line with resolution 1325, the Government ran workshops out of which it hoped to design a five-year national action plan, with support from the United Nations Development Programme (UNDP) and the United Nations Development Fund for Women (UNIFEM). Its first report to Committee on the Elimination of Discrimination against Women began this year; the country now had a platform to combat gender violence and a system for providing assistance to victims. A group of women lawyers had formed a grass-roots organization to provide advice and legal support to victims of violence.

NURBEK JEENBAEV (Kyrgyzstan), stressing that his country was combating forced marriage, said the Government had adopted the Convention on the Elimination of all Forms of Discrimination against Women in 1996 and was taking all measures to eliminate discrimination against women. However, like many countries, it had reservations. He further noted that there was a practice in Kyrgyzstan of women being abducted and forced into marriage. Indeed, when Kyrgyzstan submitted its report to the Convention's monitoring Committee, among the Committee's final observations had been a note on the problems of forced marriages.

He said that, according to sociologists, there were cases where women were abducted to marry men whose name they did not even know. Typically, these women were under 18. Kyrgyzstan's parliament had studied the issue and recently held hearings, generating a great deal of interest in the issue within Kyrgyz society. Most political parties said they were in favour of changing the legal age for marriage to 18. Of course, a court decision could mean that the age requirement was decreased to 17.

He went on to say that Kyrgyzstan had a legislative basis for protecting women's rights, particularly in the family code. Thus, the equal rights of spouses were guaranteed. To implement its obligations and to foster the principle of gender equality, the members of parliament had initiated a package of bills for gender quotas. Happily, these laws had come into force. Moreover, as Kyrgyzstan had already mentioned at the Third Committee's last session, quotas allowed women to have posts in the Government. Concluding, he affirmed that all parts of civil society and Government were carrying out awareness-raising work to address the issue of bride abductions.

GRATA WERDANINGTYAS (Indonesia), aligning herself with the Group of 77 and China, noted that, beyond commemorating the establishment of the Beijing Declaration, it was important to produce concrete strategies and actions based on lessons learned. It was also important to ensure that efforts to promote the aims of the women's anti-discrimination Convention did not distract from meeting the burden of multiple crises. It was crucial for the international community to systematically link women to development, and ensure women were a part of decision-making. At the national level, Indonesia had produced a gender responsive budget in its Government agencies. Gender focal points and working groups had been set up to strengthen coordination among them. The number of women in parliament rose from 11 per cent in 2004 to 19 per cent in 2009. The number of women entrepreneurs was also growing, with 35 per cent of small- and medium-sized enterprises being run by them. The Women Cooperative Programme for Family Welfare provided women with greater access to credit in rural areas.

She said, as women gained more opportunities in the labour market, a related phenomenon had arisen: the simultaneous increase of informal work and migration among women. While the trend was not necessarily negative, a high degree of insecurity had been associated with migrant workers in the informal sector, and more so for women. They were susceptible to violent acts from others. The Government was conducting advocacy and mediation, as well as providing legal counsel, for migrant workers abroad. It was engaging with the Governments of other countries to formulate mutually beneficial agreements on the protection of migrant workers. It was also working with the International Labour Organization to train Government officials on protection of migrants and collecting data.

She ended by emphasizing the need to accentuate the role of women in the world's efforts to reset the global economy on a more equitable path. In the long term, women's full potential could be better realized with more education and other resources at an early stage. To promote their role outside of agriculture, the world would need to promote access to credit. Further, collaboration among countries to fight violence against women migrant workers should be strengthened.

SALAMATU HUSSAINI SULEIMAN (Nigeria) aligning her statement with the one made on behalf of the Group of 77 and

China, said her country believed that full implementation of the Beijing Declaration and the other relevant international instruments was necessary to advance the national, regional and global agenda for women's empowerment. It had consistently been committed to gender mainstreaming through administrative and legal measures, as well as through the achievement of the Millennium Development Goals. Also, gender-responsive programmes were constantly being strengthened to address emerging challenges. Poverty reduction strategies had also been put in place, including the Women's Fund for Economic Empowerment. To boost women's entrepreneurship, a business development fund for women had also been established, which served as a soft-credit facility. A progressive improvement had been seen in literacy rates among women, as well as in school enrolment rates of girls and women. Among other initiatives, she highlighted a "second-chance" programme that allowed girls who had dropped out due to pregnancy to return to school.

She stressed that women continued to play an increasing role in Nigeria's ongoing political reform. Currently, the number of senior female civil servants was judged to be 22.5 per cent, while judicial appointment across the 36 States constituted about 30 per cent. A national action plan on the Promotion and Protection of Human Rights in Nigeria had been deposited with the United Nations Human Rights Councilin Geneva in July 2009. A chapter was devoted to the rights of women and children. A National Policy on Sexual Harassment in Educational Institutions had also been put in place. Free medical treatment was provided for victims of domestic and sexual violence at temporary shelters that were being established nationwide. Nigeria was also working to improve the education of girls by recruiting more female teachers, creating skill acquisition programmes for girls and women, and providing textbooks at subsidized rates, among other measures. Judges and magistrates were continuously being trained on gender and women's rights. Health system facilities were being scaled up.

Notwithstanding these achievements, a number of challenges remained, she said. Many involved the health sector, particularly in the area of ante- and post-natal care. Global partnerships and effective national coordination were critical. While a national strategy had been created to this end, improved technical and financial support from development partners remained key to improving the interest and welfare of women and girls. Nigeria supported the creation of a composite gender entity, in that regard.

SAMAR AL-ZIBDEH (Jordan), aligning herself with the Group of 77 and China, expressed support for the formation of a new gender entity and said her country would work actively to define its shape, which should perhaps be headed by an Under-Secretary General. She said her country's national priority was to promote the participation of women in politics and society. In addition, it supported the Secretary-General's campaign to end violence against women. Jordan aimed to tackle the inhumane phenomenon of trafficking in persons and had set up an ombudsman to oversee questions of discrimination and violence. It had signed 30 memorandums of understanding with various Governments and non-governmental organizations on that issue.

She said notwithstanding the thirtieth anniversary of the Women's Anti-Discrimination Convention, fifteenth of Beijing, and the tenth anniversary of the adoption of Security Council resolution 1325 (2000), the world still had a long way to go in advancing the rights of women. In addition, the fifteenth anniversary of the Cairo conference on population and development should be commemorated in such a way to shed light on women with disabilities, women living in rural areas, women who were displaced, and those living under foreign occupation. Indeed, the issue of gender equality was multisectoral; it attracted tremendous attention from all United Nations organs. Her Government looked forward to the appointment of a Secretary-General's Special Representative on combating violence against women.

HELEN HORSINGTON (Australia), speaking also on behalf of Canada and New Zealand, reaffirmed those countries commitments to, and support of, gender equality as a fundamental human right. The full participation of women in economic, social and political life was key to reducing poverty and enhancing growth and governance. It was important to enhance the life of women, girls and their families. She reaffirmed her commitment to the Beijing Platform, the forthcoming outcome of Beijing +15, the Cairo Programme of Action, and the Women's Anti-Discrimination Convention. She noted the international community's recognition of gender equality through the Millennium Development Goals, and added that gender equality and women's empowerment were goals in their own right, as well as a means to achieving the Millennium Goals.

She noted that Millennium Development Goal 5, on maternal health, was one in which countries had made the least progress. Most maternal deaths were preventable. She reminded States of their collective commitments in Cairo in 1994. Australia, Canada and New Zealand supported the recently adopted Human Rights Council resolution on preventable maternal mortality and morbidity and human rights. She welcomed increased coordination between donors on that issue, and the positive role of the World Health Organization (WHO), the United Nations Population Fund (UNFPA) and the United Nations Children's Fund (UNICEF) in that area. In March 2010, the Commission on the Status of Women would undertake a 15 year review of Beijing, embodying the international commitment to the advancement of women. She asked States to seize that opportunity to renew their commitment to the Beijing Platform and ensure equal rights for men and women. She supported the system-side coherence resolution calling for the creation of a composite gender entity, and expressed hope that it would be led by a strong and competent Under-Secretary-General. Equality was not yet won; it was time for States to take more measures to secure women's safety, economic well-being and status in society. It required active participation from both men and women.

MAHINDA SAMARASINGHE, Minister of Disaster Management and Human Rights of Sri Lanka, said the adoption of the Beijing Platform for Action and the Convention on the Elimination of Discrimination against Women were major achievements in global efforts to empower women. The Millennium Development Goals set a deadline of 2015 for providing equal opportunities for women. The Secretary-General's UNiTE campaign added impetus to efforts to ensure the protection of women in vulnerable environments. Still, violence against women remained a global challenge. For its part, Sri Lanka's constitution guaranteed equal rights to all, irrespective of gender. The Convention had been ratified and a women's charter implemented. A ministry for women's empowerment had also been established to formulate policies for social and economic empowerment programmes. Impressive gains had been made, with Sri Lanka being ranked 36 out of 155 in the Gender Development Index. Women's life expectancy rates had risen to 79 years and more women were being elected to legislative and judicial bodies.

He said programmes had been initiated to encourage women to generate income for their families by developing skills, including self-employment schemes. Today, 35 per cent of Sri Lanka's labour force was comprised of women. The Government considered combating violence against women migrant workers to be a matter of high priority. Roughly 48 per cent of the country's migrant workers were females and violence against them persisted, with undocumented women migrant workers particularly vulnerable to exploitation and discrimination. Sri Lanka strongly supported efforts by United Nations agencies to promote targeted measures, including strengthening contractual agreements, control over recruitment agencies and information campaigns, in addition to general efforts to encourage Member States to implement relevant legislation. Sri Lanka had negotiated with several countries to which migrant women were sent to ensure their welfare and protection.

As a country emerging from conflict, the Government was initiating special post-conflict programmes in its northern and eastern provinces. Many women were currently in internally displaced persons centres, where they formed over 50 per cent of the population. A National Plan of Action for the Promotion and Protection of Human Rights was being developed and would place special emphasis on women. Counselling centres had also been set up to provide psychosocial support to displaced women and girls.

KAIRE M. MBUENDE (Namibia) began by highlighting the significant strides his country made in promoting and protecting the rights of women, citing the National Gender Policy of 1997, which served to enhance the participation of women in political and decision-making processes. Women in Namibia had 30 per cent representation in Parliament, surpassing the 2005 target that was set for the Southern African Development Community (SADC) member States. The country also had 45 per cent representation of women in all regional Government councils and was working towards achieving 50 per cent female representation in parliament.

Legal reforms were made in order to address gender inequalities and redress issues of economic and social injustice brought about by discriminative cultural practices, patriarchal ideologies and historical imbalances, he said. Some of the laws included the Married Persons Equality Act, which specifies equality of persons within civil marriage and does away with the legal definition of man as head of the house. The Act also provided married women equal access to bank loans and equal power to administer joint property. The Affirmative Action (employment) Act identified affirmative action as a set of measures to ensure that all Namibians had equal employment opportunities and were equitably represented in the workforce, focusing on previously disadvantaged groups such as women and the disabled.

In terms of the Communal Land Reform Act, Namibia had made remarkable improvements in the area of the development of women in rural areas, he said. Under this law, land was to be allocated equitably and widows were given the right to remain on land allocated to their deceased husbands in rural areas, and the right to remain on the land was not affected by remarriage. On the issue of violence against women, the law entitled the Combating of Rape Act gave greater protection to young girls and boys and gave stiffer minimum sentences for rapists. The Combating of Domestic Violence Act made domestic violence a specific crime that includes physical abuse, sexual abuse, economic abuse, intimidation, harassment and emotional, verbal or psychological abuse. Those measures, including the establishment of the National Gender-Based Violence Database System, had been put in place to curb the situation.

In 2008 alone, there had been over 11,600 acts of violence against women, including assaults, attempted rape and rape, bodily harm and murders, he said. Namibia joined the international community in participating in the Secretary-General's campaign to "UNITE to End Violence against Women" and the Government also launched a media campaign on zero-tolerance against gender-based violence. Finally, Namibia had adopted other instruments to promote gender equality including: The Convention on the Elimination of All Forms of Discrimination Against Women; the Southern African Development Community (SADC) Declaration on Gender and Development; The Beijing Platform for Action; the African Charter on Women's Rights; The Protocol to the African Charter on Human and People's Rights; and the UN Convention on Transnational Organized Crime and its Protocol to prevent trafficking in persons.

JOSÉ MARIA MONTERREY SUAY (El Salvador) stressed the importance of protecting the human rights of women migrant workers, including El Salvadorian women. Improving their situation was essential to development, poverty reduction, reducing infant mortality and achieving the Millennium Development Goals.

Around 53 per cent of the population in El Salvador were women. The country had achieved gender parity in enrolment at the primary school level, and enrolment of women in secondary school and higher was higher than that of men. However, more adult women suffered from illiteracy. In the labour market, new areas had opened up for women. They were occupying higher management posts, including within the civil service. But, more domestic workers and factory workers were women, earning less than men for similar work.

He said the El Salvador Government recognized the fact that gender equality and women's empowerment were essential for attaining development. It was engaged in combating violence against women at the workplace, and was taking action against trafficking in persons. But, effective implementation of United Nations conventions and other international instruments required that State officials be properly trained. The country was currently working to ensure that was the case. Believing that gender equality was essential for democracy-building, he urged States to double their efforts to achieve the Millennium Development Goals and ensure effective compliance with international accords.

He urged the Secretary-General to continue to strengthen the role of the International Research and Training Institute for the Advancement of Women (INSTRAW) by naming a new Executive Director as soon as possible. There was a "solid correlation" between gender equality and social progress. If women did not have the same access to social, economic and cultural life, it made economies less competitive and deprived nations of essential talent.

SANJA ŠTIGLIC (Slovenia) aligned herself with the statement of the European Union and commended the Committee on the Elimination of Discrimination against Women for excellent work done in increasing the value of the anti-discrimination Convention as a most critical accountability mechanism. There had been many failures in living up to agreed upon commitments since the original adoption of the Convention thirty years ago, she said. She welcomed discussions on women's rights in the Human Rights Council and its consensually adopted resolution on the elimination of discrimination against women.

She drew attention to violence against women and girls, noting that gender-based violence was a human rights violation and had serious social and economic costs. She welcomed Security Council resolutions 1888 (2009) and 1820 (2008), specifically addressing sexual violence in the context of armed conflict and the consequences of using rape as a weapon of war. She encouraged all States that had not yet done so to sign and ratify the Statute of the International Criminal Court, which identified sexual violence in a time of war as a crime against humanity and as a war crime.

While there had been advances in addressing gender equality legislatively in Slovenia, she said, practice did not always match national standards. Ensuring a life free of gender-based violence, including domestic violence, was a substantive part of national policy. She said that domestic violence was defined as a separate criminal offence in the new penal code and that a Domestic Violence Prevention Act had been adopted last February. There were also numerous training and awareness-raising activities being developed and implemented to make violence against women socially and morally unacceptable.

MARIE YVETTE BANZON-ABALOS (Philippines) said, in August, her Government had passed the Magna Carta of Women, through which it recognized the role of Filipino women in nation-building and promoted the equality of men and women. The Magna Carta protected and promoted the rights of women in terms of political participation, economic development, justice, peace and security, as well as domestic and private life. It provided for the protection of women from all forms of violence and ensured mandatory training on human rights and gender sensitivity by all Government agents involved in the protection and defence of women against gender-based violence. Through that law, women could make legal claims against their violators and offenders.

On the subject of women migrant workers, she said a bulk of them worked at the lowest ends of the labour spectrum, often in informal manufacturing and service sectors, domestic work and entertainment. There, they suffered from gross human rights violations. Women, and migrant and domestic workers were among the first to be laid off as a result of the economic and financial crisis. Violence was being reported in free trade zones and export-processing zones, where many young women migrants were hired on temporary or insecure contracts. In light of such information, the Philippines planned to table a draft resolution on violence against women migrant workers, bringing attention to such new challenges and calling for attention to the problems of women migrant workers. She commended the Committee on the Elimination of

Discrimination against Women for its General Recommendation on women migrant workers, which recognized three categories of migrant women at high risk of abuse: women who migrated independently; women who joined their spouses who were also workers; and undocumented migrant workers. She encouraged States to report on their experience of the situation of women migrant workers, and to take heed of the Committee recommendation.

She ended by mentioning the typhoon that hit the Philippines on 26 September, pointing out the importance of gender-sensitivity in the response to emergencies and natural disasters. Also, the Philippines was committed to active participation in a discussion on the composite entity, which should provide leadership in channelling resources for gender concerns.

PAK TOK HUN (Democratic People's Republic of Korea), aligning his statement with the statement made on behalf of the Group of 77 and China, said that, with women comprising half of the world's population, it was important to bring about a proper solution for the promotion and protection of their human rights worldwide. It was particularly significant to have an in-depth deliberation on the issue of women on the thirtieth anniversary of the adoption of the Convention on the Elimination of All Forms of Discrimination against Women. His country had passed a Decree on Sex Equality in July 1946 — long before the September 1948 founding of the Democratic People's Republic of Korea — which ensured that all women enjoyed equal rights with men. Today, women exercised their full-fledged rights in all spheres of State and social life. Their status and socio-economic rights were improved each passing day under the Government's special care.

He said his delegation could not help but mention that Japan had carried out the worst kind of sexual slavery in history. It had been "hell-bent on aggression" and war in the Asian continent in the first part of the twentieth century, taking away almost 200,000 teenage girls and married women from Korea and other Asian countries as sex slaves for the Japanese army and robbing them of their human rights, chastity, and, in some cases, their lives. As that was an undeniable historical fact, it was a historical, legal and moral obligation for Japan to apologize and make a settlement for humanity. However, it had not truly reflected on, nor duly compensated, its victims. That shameless act stood in sharp contrast to the attitudes of other countries. It was not incidental that some Western countries adopted resolutions criminalizing Japan's use of "comfort women". He strongly urged Japan to make a sincere apology and a clear settlement of its dirty past.

JOEL M. NHLEKO (Swaziland), aligning his remarks with those made on behalf of the Group of 77 and China and on behalf of the Southern African Development Community, said his country was committed to the realization and full implementation of the relevant international instruments for women's empowerment, as well as regional agreements, particularly the SADC Protocol on Gender and Development, which emphasized the role women played in any society's development. Swaziland's own 1997 National Development Strategy, which was referred to as "Vision 2022", promoted gender equality as a necessary ingredient for sustainable national development. The Government recognized that rural women played a significant role in the country's socio-economic life. It further recognized the disproportionate impact on them caused by the global economic, financial, energy and food crises and by climate change. Several programmes were dedicated to empowering rural women. One example was the handcraft business Gone Rural, which employed nearly 800 women. The natural products company Swazi Secrets similarly generated income for rural Swazi women. A number of savings and credit cooperatives also catered to women.

Turning to violence against women and girls, he emphasized the huge cost of such violence to society. Physical consequences included injuries to the body, and even disability. Psychological consequences could include substance abuse, depression, anxiety, developmental delays, and eating disorders, among others. Swaziland welcomed the Secretary-General's UNiTE campaign, which aimed to end violence. A domestic bill against domestic violence would soon be passed by Swaziland's parliament and a Sexual Offences Unit had been set up in the Government. The rights of persons with disabilities were also being protected in development efforts. Further progress was needed in the areas of poverty and HIV/AIDS, particularly since women carried a triple jeopardy when it came to AIDS: as people infected with HIV, as mothers of infected children and as caregivers for those with AIDS. Swaziland was also working with its partners in SADC to combat human trafficking and supported steps taken toward the establishment of the United Nations global action plan to combat human trafficking.

SHRI BHARTRUHARI MAHTAB (India) said that the global crisis had had a disproportionately adverse impact on developing countries, even though they had not contributed to it. Within that disproportionate impact, women had been most seriously affected. Although countries had undertaken domestic responses to tackle that situation, the need for international cooperation and increased bilateral and multilateral financial assistance programmes for developing countries could not be overemphasized. Empowering women politically, educationally, economically and legally had been a major objective of India's Government. The Ministry of Women and Child Development was trying to achieve holistic empowerment of women through microcredit and support systems, such as working women's hostels. One particularly successful scheme had been the "self-help" programme, which helps create economically sustainable self-help groups. More than 2.2 million such groups, covering 33 million households, had been created.

Since its independence, India had given women equal voting rights, the representative continued, and 33 per cent of the seats in urban and local self-government had been reserved for women. In that way, more than one million women had been given a voice at the grass-roots level. Most ministries and departments had put in place gender budgeting, which helped monitor and implement policies and programmes meant to benefit women. The flip side of empowerment of women was the rampant problem of exploitation and violence against women. Apart from efforts to punish the perpetrators of such crimes, India was also taking steps to rehabilitate victims and strengthen the legal system to prevent such crimes. The most recent initiative was the "National Campaign on Prevention of Violence against Women (2009-2015), launched on 2 October, the 140th birthday of Mahatma Gandhi.

ANTHONY ANDANJE (Kenya), aligning himself with the Group of 77 and China, underscored the pivotal role played by women in the country's development. The Government had created a Ministry of Gender, Children and Social Development, as well as a National Commission of Gender and Development, to implement the national policy on gender. It had also appointed gender officers in ministries and State corporations. Through the national strategic plan — Vision 2030 — the Government had set out a strategy to increase opportunities for women's participation in economic, social and political decision-making. There was a 30 per cent quota on women's participation in political parties. A Women's Enterprise Fund provided women with access to financial services. The Government was enacting laws to counter cultural attitudes, such as the law of succession act, which provided for the right of women to inherit property that was inaccessible under customary law.

He said the sexual offences act and the family protection bill both provided women with protection against violence. The Government was also working with civil society and community-based organizations to foster a change in the attitudes that condoned the abuse of women's rights and inequalities between men and women. A witness protection programme provided immunity to witnesses in legal proceedings, in light of the fact that many female victims of violence did not seek legal recourse for fear of reprisals. A forthcoming marriage bill and matrimonial property bill would further promote women's rights. Efforts were also being made to eradicate female genital mutilation, with the Government making interventions through community elders to declare support for the abandonment of that practice. Also, because two-thirds of people infected by HIV were women, the Government was working to ensure that women had equitable access to anti-retroviral treatment, while at the same time making sure to stem mother-child transmission of HIV/AIDS. He ended by calling for "expedited intergovernmental discussions" on the new gender architecture at the United Nations, acknowledging the invaluable work of UNIFEM, UNDP, UNFPA and the Joint United Nations Programme on HIV/AIDS (UNAIDS) in Kenya.

SANDRA SIMOVICH (Israel) welcomed the Secretary-General's report on violence against women, singling out it's initiative "UNiTE to End Violence against Women" as well as others concerned with capacity-building for States that might be willing to fight gender based violence, but lacked expertise and resources. She also praised recent Security Council resolutions concerning sexual violence against women in conflict situations, the most recent of which Israel had co-sponsored. The appointment of a Special Representative on the issue should help focus the international community on those abhorrent acts. She further expressed support for the adoption by the General Assembly of resolution 63/311 calling for the creation of a single, coherent gender entity, which had resulted from consultations on system-wide coherence.

Noting a number of achievements by Israeli women stemming from guarantees of social and political rights in Israel's Declaration of Independence, she said that the greatest advancements for women were in the legislative field. As an example, she cited a 2007 law requiring that all proposed legislation be examined for potential gender implications, as well as one passed last year providing financial incentives to employers who modified work conditions to meet the needs of women and parents, among other legislative activities. She further noted the advancement of Arab women in Israel that had resulted, among other things, in increased enrolment of Arab women in higher education from 40 per cent of all Arab students a decade ago to 60 per cent in 2006.

For societies in conflict, women often provided continuity and sanity, she said. In that spirit, some Israeli and Palestinian women were working to bring peace closer through a series of seminars entitled "Women Building a New Reality: a Dialogue between Israeli and Palestinian Women," which brought together some 25 Palestinian and Israeli women at each event for intensive programs of debate, discussion, soul-searching and forging friendships. Eighteen such seminars had taken place to date. "These seminars might seem small steps," she said, "but in the area of confidence building, perception changing, and women's empowerment, every step counts and no step is too small," she said.

GERARD VINLUAN (Singapore) said Singapore's Women's Everest team climbed Mount Everest this year, which was a testament to their courage, determination and empowerment. The climb was also a mirror of the journey through life for many women in Singapore. The Government had put in place legal and institutional safeguards to ensure that women were able to access education and health care, and contribute to the nation in an atmosphere that was safe, stable and supportive. The Government regularly reviewed the employment act, penal code and women's charter to improve the position, rights and protection of women, and it demonstrated its support of women's advancement by acceding to the Women's Anti-Discrimination Convention in 1995.

He noted that Singapore ranked 16 out of 182 countries in 2007 in terms of equality of opportunity for men and women, rising from 18 in 2006. It had a high literacy rate for women, and more women were going to university. Representation in parliament had risen for women, and Singapore was ranked 21 out of 187 countries in terms of percentage of women in the lower house of Government. There were 5 female political office-holders and 17 female members of parliament. More women in Singapore were climbing the corporate ladder, with three of them listed in the Financial Times' Top 50 women business leaders in the world. To empower women, the Government was creating viable work options that harmonized women's family and work commitments. Among its initiatives was the "30 Minutes to Work" programme, which matched non-working women with jobs located close to home. The income gap had narrowed in Singapore, with women now earning 91.8 per cent of what men earned.

MAGDALENA GRABIANOWSKA (Poland) said her Government aligned itself with the statement by the European Union. But, she wished to reiterate the understanding that references to the sexual and reproductive rights of women in the statement by the European Union did not constitute "an encouragement of the promotion of abortion."

DAMIANO BELEFFI (San Marino) said his country attached great importance to the promotion and protection of human rights, with special attention to the most vulnerable groups of persons, such as children, disabled persons, older persons and women. It endorsed the United Nations' commitment to women's rights and strongly supported the Secretary-General's UNiTE campaign.

He recalled his country's active participation in debates on the responsibility to protect populations from genocide, war crimes, crimes against humanity and ethnic cleansing, an issue that included the responsibility to protect women and girls from mass rapes and mutilations. Nationally, the Government was part of the Council of Europe's campaign to combat violence against women, including domestic violence. It sponsored a television spot about violence against women. A special hotline, Telefono Rosa, provided legal, medical and psychological support to victims of violence. At the international level, the United Nations was essential for promoting the advancement of women as a matter of principle and a matter of economic growth, poverty reduction and development.

ESRAQ ABDULLAH HAMMAD (Yemen) said the third Committee represented an important forum for discussing challenges facing women and fashioning solutions to advance their situation. She noted the various relevant international agreements and outcome documents that guided the Committee's efforts and stressed that national, regional and international efforts must be rededicated and redoubled to improve the status of women. In this regard, Yemen reaffirmed its obligations. It had been one of the first countries to sign the Convention on the Elimination of All Forms of Discrimination against Women and continued to submit its country reports. At the same time, it had introduced a number of amendments to national laws related to women to align them with its international commitments. Most recently it had, with the passage of the personal status law, raised the national age for marriage to 17.

She said a number of departments were also set up to deal with women's rights. National strategies and development plans, particularly one aimed at advancing women during the period from 2006 to 2016, had been created. Overall, these steps testified to Yemen's commitment to furthering the advancement of women. Yemeni women had already achieved success at all levels and all areas of society. The promotion and participation of women in public affairs had been standardized within the President's political initiative for reform, which will be implemented beginning next year. Among other things, that initiative aimed to raise the proportion of women in Parliament to 15 per cent. Concluding, she reiterated her country's concern for the suffering of Palestinian women.

OLHA KAVUN (Ukraine), aligning herself with the European Union, said gender equality was not only an end in itself, but also a means to development. The principle of gender equality was exercised when ensuring equal representation of women and men in decision-making, the representation of women at senior levels of legislative and executive bodies, and in outlining and implementing policies and programmes at the United Nations itself. The Ukraine would submit its report to the Committee on the Elimination of Discrimination against Women in 2010, in which it was expected to report on progress in establishing mechanisms to ensure equal rights and opportunities for both sexes. She encouraged other States to submit overdue reports, but also added that the Committee should produce "combined documents," particularly when dealing with "non-initial reports".

She noted that 95 per cent of the victims of family violence were women, and that, in the Ukraine, there were 150 Governmental and non-governmental organizations devoted to assisting victims. Ukraine was a strong supporter of the Secretary-General's UNiTecampaign, and was running its own campaign against violence towards women called "Stop Violence!" From 1 to 4 million persons fell victim to human trafficking, among them the women and children of Ukraine. Its Government was deeply concerned about the links between organized crime and human trafficking, drug trafficking and terrorism. The Government strongly supported the United Nations Global Initiative to Fight Human Trafficking, and stood ready to enhance its cooperation with others to fight that scourge. She noted that trafficking flourished in areas of armed conflict, where the majority of refugees and displaced persons were women and children.

A. K. ABDUL MOMEN (Bangladesh), aligning himself with the Group of 77 and China, flagged several issues of importance from his national perspective. Bangladesh had always been at the forefront of gender mainstreaming, gender equality and the advancement of women. It was a State Party to almost all the major international instruments relating to women's rights. In 1998, a national plan of action was drawn up for 15 ministries, departments and agencies, with progress monitored by the Women's Development Implementation Committee, headed by the Minister of Women and Children's Affairs. The Government had invested heavily in women's education, resulting in gender parity in primary and secondary school enrolment.

The situation of women in rural areas had improved dramatically as a result of Bangladesh's successful microcredit programme, with women becoming agents of change, he continued. In urban areas, women pursued jobs in the garment or ceramics industries, thus achieving financial freedom. In terms of political empowerment, women in Bangladesh enjoyed prominent representation in various decision-making posts in important ministries, such as the ministries of defence, energy, foreign affairs, home affairs and agriculture, which were all headed by women.

Achieving gender equality was an agonizingly slow process, he said, since it touched on one of the most deeply entrenched human attitudes. Changing those attitudes required beefing up public awareness on discriminatory behavioural patterns and stereotypes.

He encouraged the United Nations to mainstream a gender perspective into actions relating to climate change, the food and energy crises, food security and all deliberation at major United Nations conferences and summits. In that respect, Bangladesh welcomed the adoption of the decision to establish a composite gender entity. His Government had integrated a gender perspective in United Nations peacekeeping, by committing to provide a female formed police unit. The Peace building Commission had considered human rights and gender equality in its country-specific work, which was encouraging. The Commission should also implement Security Council resolution 1325 fully. He also urged developed countries to fulfil their official development assistance commitments, a due portion of which was used for activities relating to the empowerment of women.

ONON SODOV, Director of the Department of International Organizations, Ministry of Foreign Affairs and Trade of Mongolia, aligning her statement with the one made on behalf of the Group of 77 and China, reaffirmed her country's strong commitment to fully implementing the Beijing Declaration and Platform for Action. The issues of gender equality and women's empowerment, including access to education and skills training, full employment, affordable pubic health care services and ending all forms of violence against women were key factors for social development and achievement of the Millennium Development Goals.

She said Mongolia had taken comprehensive measures to ensure gender equality and women's empowerment. Several key policy documents had been approved and substantial progress had been made in implementing them. The establishment of the National Committee for Gender Equality, which was headed by Mongolia's Prime Minister, was particularly important, in that regard. However, much more needed to be done in the areas of poverty reduction, decreasing urban and rural disparities, reducing violence against women and girls, and increasing the leadership capacity of women. The situation of women in rural areas also deserved special attention. Efforts had been made to support them through income generating activities, including the provision of small, low interest loans, better health services and skills training. In this, particular emphasis was given to poor women and female-headed households.

G. SEDDIQ RASULI (Afghanistan) noted that eight years had passed since the signing of the Bonn Agreement on Afghanistan. In that time, the Government had made advances in various sectors, including education, health and institution-building. Since the collapse of the Taliban, Afghanistan had seen the re-employment of women in Government and the resumption of female education. Women had also begun participating at broad and unprecedented levels in the political, social, economic and cultural life of Afghanistan. The country had a Ministry of Women's Affairs, and was fully committed to human rights, women's empowerment and gender equality, which were provided for in the Constitution.

As part of Afghanistan's national development strategy, launched in June 2008, the Government had established benchmarks to measure progress on the advancement of women, he said. It had set a deadline of 2010 to achieve gender equality, including the participation of women in politics and society, providing legal privileges for women, and implementing a national action plan for women's development. In the most recent elections, two women ran for President and seven ran for Vice President. Some 328 women ran for provincial council seats. Of the 4.5 million new voters, 38 per cent were women. About 41 per cent of students enrolled in primary and secondary school were girls, 20 per cent of those enrolled at universities were women, and 75 per cent of students attending literacy courses were women. But, the "enemies of the people and Government" were burning down schools and insecurity was affecting the engagement of women in education and other productive activities. The Government had criminalized violence against women. Working with UNIFEM, the Ministry of Women's Affairs reviewed cases involving violence against women to better address claims of violence.

GUSTAVO MENES (Argentina), aligning himself with the Group of 77 and China and the Rio Group, said the elimination of violence against women was indispensable to the full and equal participation of women in society. In March, the Argentine Congress enacted a law on the eradication of violence against women, with sanctions against perpetrators. That law was in line with recommendations by the Committee on the Elimination of Discrimination against Women. The national campaign for gender equality — under the slogan "Another life is possible; we have the right to a life without violence," — saw the participation of

Government, international organizations and non-governmental organizations. National programmes also existed to protect migrant workers from gender-based violence, irrespective of their migrant status. The Government was conducting training and awareness-raising among members of the security forces on how to handle violence against women.

He said Argentina attached special attention to improving the situation of women in rural areas. The countries of the Southern Common Market (MERCOSUR) had convened a thematic group on gender, in the context of the special meeting on family agriculture. That group would work to ensure that rural women had equal access to land, and would be educated on their rights. Argentina's laws guaranteed unrestricted access to education, justice and other forms of protection to migrants, as well. Indeed, its Constitution declared that "all inhabitants are equal before the law and have to be accepted for employment based solely on capabilities".

On the new composite gender entity, he expressed hope that debates on that would be open and transparent. The four gender entities should be allowed to actively participate in defining the parameters of that entity, so that the new mechanism would reflect the capabilities, knowledge and resources inherent in each of them.

MANAR YACOUB BAHLIJI (Bahrain) stressed that the empowerment of women was a main goal of the Millennium Development Goals. The international community was exerting efforts to this end, thereby underscoring the statement made during the Beijing conference that advancing the status of women was a collective responsibility. Bahrain had a special interest in granting women all their political rights, particularly by allowing them to stand for political office. Great achievements were made in that regard during the 2002 and 2006 elections. Moreover, Bahrain was chosen for the establishment of a centre to promote women's economic leadership, which allowed it to make greater progress in advancing women's empowerment.

She stressed her Government's wish to further the status of women in all fields. It had taken the Millennium Development Goals as a framework for that effort. Most recently, the rehabilitation of women had been called for in building up the State. Moreover, a national strategy for the promotion of women was raising awareness of women's rights. Other tracks aimed to increase women's economic empowerment and protect the family. On 27 May 2009, Bahrain's king issued Act 19 of 2009 on family provisions, as part of the national campaign to preserve that social institution. A symposium was also held on family law. Bahrain had made strides to provide better access to education and health services, which was reflected in the analysis of the country in the Human Development Report from UNDP.

NAZEK SHAWISH (Libya) reaffirmed her country's commitment to the Beijing Declaration and other agreements whose objectives were related to the advancement of women. Libya believed in equality between male and female citizens in their duties and responsibilities. Its law was based on Qur'anic tenets stressing the importance of freedom from slavery. Education was considered a ticket to paradise. A woman had a right to choose her husband, and she did not have to change her name upon marriage. She came with a dowry and had the right to an independent sum of money. Women carried out responsibilities just like men. Libyan women had made progress in protecting rights and participating in decision-making. They had posts in the legal field, police, army and other occupations. Women were present at all levels of education. The number of students at university in 2007-2008 was 1.93 million, of which 500,000 were women. The number of girls exceeded the number of boys in secondary and primary education.

She expressed concern about the situation of Palestinian women under Israeli occupation. She condemned the ongoing violations of the Zionist occupying forces for the psychological suffering they inflicted on Palestinian women, and for the crimes they had committed in Gaza, and elsewhere in the occupied territory, as described in the recent report to the Human Rights Council. She also expressed concern over the worsening situation of African women, due to poverty, hunger, illnesses and armed conflict, which had hampered their participation in development. Libya was enabling women in African countries through a health care programme it had established with Nigeria and Cuba. She urged the international community to seriously condemn the trafficking of women, which was a crime against humanity. She expressed satisfaction with UNIFEM's efforts to bring its activities in line with the Millennium Development Goals.

ABDUL GHAFOOR MOHAMED (Maldives) said his country was encouraged by the increased attention given to addressing gaps in gender equality by the United Nations. He welcomed the recent statement from the Security Council calling for the full participation of women in all stages of conflict resolution and peace building. More importantly, by unanimously adopting resolution 1888 (2009), it had called for immediate action to protect civilians, including women and children from all forms of sexual violence. At the national level, the Maldives continued to empower its women, and its attempts to institutionalize gender equality in recent years had proved successful. The traditional gender bar that had prevented women from competing for the office of president had been removed in the new constitution. The equal-pay-for-equal-work policy ensured that wage gaps did not exist.

He stressed, however, that the journey to full institutional and de jure equality for women in all aspects of life looked long and daunting. Mainstreaming gender equality in the development agenda required extensive institutional advancements. Although women in the Maldives were among the most emancipated in the Muslim world, the mixed effects of globalization on the island nation's fragile economy had widened gender disparities. For example, geography and culture posed challenges for women in taking up employment in the booming tourism industry. Moreover, the Maldives was starting to experience the negative effects of extremism. The marriage of underage girls was now an emerging issue in society. Economic and social constraints still restricted women from simultaneously pursuing the dual worlds of private and public life.

Against that backdrop, and as the thirtieth anniversary of the Convention on the Elimination of All Forms of Discrimination against Women was celebrated, the Government of the Maldives was focused on erasing laws that prevented women's advancement and enacting judicial reform, he said. International technical cooperation would, however, be needed. Additionally, a concerted effort to reform the global economy was needed, to ensure the achievement of the Millennium Development Goals.

FEDERICO ALBERTO CUELLO CAMILO (Dominican Republic), aligning himself with the Group of 77 and China and the Rio Group, said it was not possible to achieve development or to raise the level of welfare of society without improving the health, education, social and political participation and economic development of women. In terms of health, his Government had a strategic plan aimed at reducing the incidence of

HIV/AIDS, and reducing maternal mortality was a national priority. It had several laws, plans, programmes and projects giving special attention to the advancement of women in education, social, health, political participation and economic empowerment, with a view towards achieving true equity and equality between men and women.

He said the Dominican Republic was the host country of INSTRAW, which was a research and training centre on gender issues. Only INSTRAW had that mandate within the United Nations. Research and training on gender issues was pertinent to a developing country such as the Dominican Republic. It was in that spirit that the Assembly selected a developing country as the location of INSTRAW's headquarters. Moving the tasks of research and training to a developed country would deviate from the Assembly's mandate. He said he trusted that intergovernmental negotiations on system-wide coherence would conclude with the establishment of a solid entity that "fully gathered" the mandate of each of the four gender institutions at the United Nations. The new entity should preserve the mandates of those institutions, and in that way, preserve the specific and unique mandate of INSTRAW as a tool for advancing the status of women.

ROBLE OLHAYE (Djibouti), aligning himself with the Group of 77 and China, noted, like others, that despite impressive progress, women continued to be disproportionately affected by food insecurity, hunger, poverty, disasters and crises. They also suffered from unspeakable violence. It was perplexing that an increasing number of peacekeeping soldiers, sent to restore law and order, were themselves responsible for such criminal behaviour. There was an urgent need to adopt a zero-tolerance policy for violence perpetrated against women by United Nations peacekeepers. Gender-based and sexual violence must be eliminated from situations of armed conflict and in times of humanitarian emergencies.

He said the international community needed to examine the positive role of women in economic development. Investing in women and girls had a multiplier effect on production, efficiency and sustained economic growth. It was difficult to point out any country that had achieved development without the strong participation of women at all levels. Policies aimed at decent work and full employment for each citizen should include measures to

promote gender equality and women's empowerment. That included removing structural and legal barriers, and promoting equal pay for equal work. In that respect, he welcomed the adoption of a resolution on system-wide coherence that included a provision for the establishment of a single gender entity. Equally, he welcomed Security Council resolution 1888 (2009) that called on the appointment of a Special Representative on sexual violence in armed conflict. He encouraged States to meet the goal of funding the United Nations Trust Fund to Eliminate Violence against Women.

Right of Reply

Speaking in exercise of the right of reply to the statement made by the delegation of the Democratic People's Republic of Korea, Japan's representative said the remarks had been unclear. It sounded as if Japan refused to face its past. But that was not true. Regarding comfort women, the Government had extended in a statement made on 4 August 1993 its sincere remorse. Moreover, in the Japan-Pyongyang Declaration of 2002, it was clearly mentioned that the Japanese side acknowledged that it had caused suffering on the Korean peninsula during its colonial past.

Regarding the settlement of the issue between Japan and the Democratic People's Republic of Korea, Japan had held talks on this as part of the broader talks on normalizing relations between the two countries. It would continue to do so. Further, Prime Minister Hatoyama had stated, in his remarks during the General Assembly's general debate, his Government's desire to settle all issues with the Democratic People's Republic of Korea. Today, the Japanese delegation wished to remind the Democratic People's Republic of Korea to take steps toward the normalization of relations, which would include an acknowledgement of the past.

The representative of the United States said his delegation regretted the use of the word "genocide" by Cuba yesterday to describe his country's actions. This was an inappropriate use of the term. While the United States had a blockade against Cuba, it was also the largest provider of food to Cuba. It also exported medicine and medical equipment to that country and was Cuba's fifth largest trading partner. The United States had taken a number of steps in recent months to facilitate family travel, and to lift restrictions on remittances. It had also resumed talks on migration and the resumption of mail services with Cuba. Further, the United States had issued over 120 visas to persons visiting the intelligence operatives mentioned by the Cuban delegation.

Responding to Japan, the representative of the Democratic People's Republic of Korea said his statement had been based on historical facts and there should be no lack of clarity. Indeed, all of those facts showed that Japan had not sincerely admitted its past crimes, particularly with respect to the 200,000 women it had abducted. Japan's position concerning this issue differed from time to time and place to place. All the words and acts of the Japanese concerning the comfort women showed that they refused to admit their responsibility. Over the years, various officials had made "reckless remarks" that there was no evidence proving the forcible recruitment of these comfort women or statements that there had been no comfort women, only prostitutes sold by their parents. More recently, on 23 July 2009 in this very room, the Japanese delegation had said, during its presentation to the Committee on the Elimination of Discrimination against Women, that the comfort women issue had been settled.

He said his delegation was concerned about how Japan would present itself in the future when no witnesses were living. Indeed, there was no assurance that the shameful past would not be repeated in Japan's case. He urged Japan to address its past wrongdoings, for its own sake.

The representative of Cuba, replying to the representative of the United States, said she had thought he would announce the granting of a visa to the wife of Gerardo Hernández, one of the Cuban Five detained in America. She had thought that he would announce the immediate lifting of the trade embargo on Cuba. It was unfortunate that no such announcements had been made. In fact, the United States Department of State had never granted a single visa to Adriana Pérez O'Connor. She had never visited her husband, detained since 1998, and had been denied visas on 10 occasions.

United States authorities alleged that Ms. Pérez was a threat to national security, she said. And yet, they allowed Luis Posada Carriles, a terrorist, to freely walk the streets of Miami. An ex-CIA agent, he had admitted responsibility for an airplane attack that killed 63 passengers and crew, and a hotel bombing attack where one Italian had died. He had conspired to blow up an auditorium at a university in Cuba where President Fidel Castro was to have delivered a speech. Indeed, the delegate had not sought to explain the reason why a visa had not been granted.

As for the embargo, it remained in place, she said. Trade restrictions on Cuba remained. It was an act of aggression and genocide, according to the Geneva Conventions, and needed to be lifted. If the United States President were to do so, funds in Cuba belonging to third party countries would no longer be forfeited or frozen. Ships that had been to Cuba would cease to be seized. Financial entities would begin trading with Cuba. As recently as a few weeks ago, a Dutch company, Phillips, was informed that it could not sell medical products to Cuba due to the embargo. She urged other States to support Cuba's upcoming resolution aimed at ending the embargo.

The representative of Japan, replying to the representative of the Democratic People's Republic of Korea, repeated once more that his country was facing up to its past with sincerity and consistency. It felt remorse for its actions and had been offering apologies since the end of World War II. It had devoted 60 years to the promotion of peace, democracy and human rights. As for the issue of comfort women, his country recognized that their existence was an act involving military authorities of the day, and which injured the honour and dignity of many women, for which Japan apologized. On that issue, his country's stance remained unchanged. No country had a perfect record for its human rights situation, and Japan was no exception. But, it was unfair for it to receive criticism from a country that had no regard or respect for human rights at all. It was not possible to justify the Democratic People's Republic of Korea's ongoing violations by hiding behind the past. That country must face the reality of its human rights situation, which continued to be serious. It should protect its people's right to food, and not punish those who had left the country once they had returned. It should end public executions.

The representative of the Democratic People's Republic of Korea asked again how long it would take for Japan to sincerely redress its past crimes. To honestly settle its criminal past meant to win the world's trust and to become a member of international community with clean hands and a clean conscience.

11. Public sector banks are the backbone of Indian rural economy since private sector banks only focus on profit maximization.
12. Indian Bureaucracy needs to be more accountable to the public otherwise it will not be empathetic to the problems of Indian people.
13. Wind power Vs Solar Energy?

14. Is government just renaming the old schemes?
15. How useful is the Moderation policy in CBSE?
16. Cultural reforms, Strict laws or Educational Reform what is more important for Women Empowerment?
17. Should Capital Punishment be abolished?
18. How can we improve our performance in Rio Olympics?
19. In what way Payment Banks are useful?
20. What will be the impact of GST on Indian Economy?
21. How does US Presidential Elections affect us?
22. Air Traffic Controllers should be more concerned about the safety of passengers.
23. Fasal Bima Yojna.
24. In what way Beti Bachao Beti Padhao scheme helped our society?
25. Smart cities in India.
26. Impacts of Man Ki Baat?
27. Educational System in India is suitable or needs modification?
28. SAARC conferences.
29. Should India have One Child Policy?
30. How is 7th pay commission making government employees more responsible?
31. How helpful is the Demonetarization Drive?
32. South China Sea is an area where India should focus more now rather than Pakistan.
33. Surgical Strike issues?
34. What is the role of Social Media?
35. Are gold investments profitable?
36. Beauty contests degrade womanhood?
37. Food bill – is it really something India needs?
38. Is inflation always harmful?
39. Is underemployment more harmful than unemployment?
40. Hard work or Smart work what is important?

❑❑❑